Unlocking Liberalism

Life after the Coalition

edited by

– ROBERT BROWN, GILLIAN GLOYER
AND NIGEL LINDSAY –

An environmentally friendly book printed and bound in England by
www.printondemand-worldwide.com

Mixed Sources
Product group from well-managed
forests, and other controlled sources
www.fsc.org Cert no. TT-COC-002641
© 1996 Forest Stewardship Council
FSC

PEFC Certified
This product is
from sustainably
managed forests
and controlled
sources
PEFC
PEFC/16-33-415
www.pefc.org

This book is made entirely of chain-of-custody materials

i

FastPrint Publishing

www.fast-print.net/store.php

Unlocking Liberalism – Life after the Coalition
Copyright © Robert Brown, Gillian Gloyer and Nigel Lindsay 2014

A catalogue record for this book is available from the British Library

ISBN 978-178456-091-1

First published 2014 by
FASTPRINT PUBLISHING
Peterborough, England.

"We can shape the future of mankind, not just in Scotland, but on this planet. It is a future which could be bleak and Orwellian, but if opportunities are taken and people made aware, there is a future which glitters like rivers of molten gold."

\- Russell Johnston

Contents

Foreword

Rt Hon Charles Kennedy, MP

I'm not sure that a phoenix arising from the ashes is quite the most appropriate phrase for a compilation written pre-referendum but only appearing in its aftermath. Far less the context of the May 2015 general election. But allow me to develop the thought...

Like many another Scottish Liberal Democrat I was pretty down in the dumps politically after the 2011 Scottish elections. The inestimable Robert Brown – one of its most cruel victims – invited me to risk a very small degree of guilt by association by endorsing the thrust behind the publication of a collection of essays along the lines of the "Where do we go from here?" variety. So I did. And, at that year's party conference in Inverness, I slunk into the back of the smaller theatre to hear what was being said at the fringe meeting associated with the "The Little Yellow Book" appearing on the scene.

I came away more than encouraged. The most important impression was deeply reassuring: that instead of emerging from adversity in a welter of introspective recrimination we were still more than capable of looking outwards and forwards, imaginative and ideas-driven. That's the mindset and motive-force which shall more than see us through the post-referendum scenario and the 2015 Westminster general election.

The ideas which follow are designed to help feed into the 2016 Scottish Holyrood manifesto process but also to contribute to the wider Liberal Democrat debate across the UK as to our role and purpose as the Parliament of the Coalition nears its end. As Robert put it to me "to help develop a narrative, themes and policy ideas from a radical Liberal perspective." Ideas which know no institutional or geographic boundaries rooted in values which we all share in this happily disputatious political family. The ferment of ideas is proof positive of political life – fickle and fun. It is neither my role nor intent here to endorse or disavow – just to encourage healthy exchange.

One matter in the current considerable political swirl does at least seem fairly clear: the Scottish parliament is set to accrue further powers in due course. A challenge for us surely is to ensure that the process of more power to the Edinburgh tier does not stop there. We need to be viewing our ideas and policies in a way that enables them to be far more rooted at a city, regional and community level, as well as looking to the future shape and priorities of the UK.

In power the SNP government has pulled power to the centre – at times to an extent which would have made even Mrs Thatcher baulk. Just look at what has happened to our emergency services, not least the police. And see the effrontery by which my home and highly distinctive area of the Highlands & Islands has seen the erosion of powers to the centre at the expense of such distinctive and long-standing institutions as Highlands & Islands Enterprise and the Crofting Commission.

Apart from seeking to reverse such an unwelcome trend we must devise strategies to strongly encourage if not ensure that future powers and policies are more localised across Scotland – a kind of tartan federalism within and across our diverse nation should beckon. The neat political footwork of both the Northern and Western Isles can help show the rest of us the way. Let's not stop there – should not that David Steel nod in the direction of "city states" not find greater application? And how about revisiting the notion of directly elected Mayors for our cities and regions? We need counterbalance to the Central Belt, just as much as we need rebalance where the South East of England is concerned.

This summer demonstrated such power – when properly coordinated – as Glasgow staged the Commonwealth Games. Edinburgh demonstrates it annually with the Festival (let us set the trams issue in a curious category of its own, for these purposes); Aberdeen is a global energy centre; Dundee has consolidated its reputation in the field of cutting edge technologies. And all boast truly international universities. There is much here – yet still on a comparatively small size of canvas – to build upon where fresh thinking is concerned. But already I have strayed well beyond my remit in this Preface.

Note also that this collection of thought-provoking essays contains contributions from outside the membership ranks of the Liberal Democrats. Let that be a template for our wider political conduct into the uncertain waters ahead. We have always been at our best – and prospered politically – when we have been able to pursue just such a course – witness over the decades our stances on everything from Hong Kong citizens' passport rights to green growth, student support to Iraq.

That essence must be recaptured because it is not on offer anywhere else in Scottish and UK politics. It is grounded in our instinctive sense of radicalism and an inherent understanding that if we're not prepared to live a little dangerously then the greater threat is that we end up not living at all.

Read, reflect – and react!

Charles Kennedy

The Setting – A Future with a Flawed Prospectus

Robert Brown

The Banking Collapse

The banking collapse of 2008 has probably been one of the most significant events since the war, ranking along with the Cuban missile crisis and the fall of the Berlin Wall. Its effects – economic, financial, social and political – will take decades to work through and how this legacy is tackled will mark the life chances of this and perhaps future generations.

What are these effects?

The *economic effects* are the most obvious and possibly the most profound. The growing personal wealth of most people in most Western countries – modest in most cases, massive for those at the top – turned out to be partly fuelled by an unsustainable bubble in the financial services sector and the housing market. As it stalled, it hit the living standards of average families and reduced the funding available to the State to support public services and social security for the poor. Oddly the effects on employment were far less than predicted, possibly because of the contemporaneous trend towards more people in jobs living on poverty wages – the "working poor".

The collapse of the Royal Bank of Scotland led to the famous description of Scotland by Vince Cable as "a large bank with a small country attached". But the reality is that the market constraints which allow the system to be cleansed by bankruptcy of unsuccessful or outmoded businesses with limited damage to the wider economy no longer work when companies can juggle or eliminate their tax liabilities across national boundaries, can take over other companies on "tick" and then asset strip both the company and its workforce, or when they are simply too big to be allowed to fail.

The *financial effects* are inter-generational. The era of inflation proof pensions, generalised growing wealth and increasing funding for public services has ended, certainly for some years. Instead governments across the western world juggle with large and unbalanced public finances which are generally agreed to be a burden on future generations unless they can be reduced to more manageable proportions.

The banks remain fearful and partly dysfunctional in their primary role of supporting domestic and small business customers. Savers cannot get an economic interest rate which beats inflation while historically low borrowing rates are not the economic stimulus they once were because people are frightened both to lend and to borrow.

The *social effects* are the most challenging. They are not as such caused by the banking collapse but by other longer standing consequences of the dysfunctionality of our society – growing inequality within many countries (although perhaps not, as Professor Tyler Cowen points out[1], on a global scale where economic trends have narrowed inequality); a steady growth of political and social disengagement and distrust amongst the population at large; reduced opportunities for a decent job for a significant

---

[1] Prof. Tyler Cowen - article in The New York Times 19th July 2014

percentage of young people, particularly boys for whom the traditional careers in traditional heavy industries are no longer there; the emergence of two new strata in society – the working poor operating at subsistence level, sometimes on and out of jobs, and dependent to a considerable degree on the benefits system – and an underclass of people damaged by drug and alcohol addiction, mental or physical health problems or lack of self worth or opportunity. The working poor and the underclass of course overlap with each other and with broader society.

Finally *the political effects*. These are shown in the deterioration in the level of much political discourse; the rise of political parties and movements across Europe which seek structural change based on hatred of either the existing state/institution or of the perceived dominant elites; the lack of effective political choices; and the decline of support for the general public interest.

In Scotland, the banking crisis together with other developments have led to a crisis of the state – the United Kingdom – and a referendum which has major implications (only dimly recognised as yet in England) for the whole of Britain. But, although social attitude studies have identified that Scottish attitudes towards contemporary social issues are pretty similar to attitudes across the rest of the UK, the alienation from government which underlies the political success of the SNP has taken a somewhat different form in the hands of Alex Salmond and the Nationalists to that which has fed the advance of UKIP across Britain as a whole.

Wrong Directions

There is a strong case for saying that much of current political and economic theory is pointing in the wrong direction. There has been no real national debate about the moral and political lessons of 2008. What became of traditional prudential banking ethics? How can the national economy collapse but no one goes to jail? Who can control

9

the unacceptable face of capitalism when it is displayed on a global stage?

Any sensible discourse would question the idea that anyone needs an annual income in excess of £1 million, yet thousands of top executives and city whizz kids wallow in obscene wealth – like some demented economic version of the mile high club.

Success and failure are measured in terms of GDP not of anything remotely linked to human happiness or success. If an oil tanker spills millions of tons of oil on the sea, any rational person would observe that resources are wasted and costs incurred – yet the clean-up costs actually add to GDP. If there is a shortage of housing, the costs of house purchase go up and GDP is again increased. On any view, GDP as a proxy for social welfare is a highly flawed measure – GDP in accounting terms is an estimate of the costs instead of the benefits of all market-related economic activities.[2] The Coalition government asked the National Statistics Office to look at GDP and whether there could be better indicators developed, while the Scottish government have also been closely interested in the issue. As yet, the alternatives have their own problems but we cannot ignore the importance of measuring the success of economies in other ways than GDP and we need to keep thinking about how to do it at the forefront.

And the insights of the authors of *The Spirit Level*[3] (pursued by a tremendous essay in this book by Duncan Exley, the current Director of the Equality Trust) – that more unequal societies are less happy, with growing

---

[2] Evaluating Alternatives to GDP as Measures of Social Welfare/Progress – Jeroen C.J.M. van den Bergh and Miklos Anital - European Commission European Research Area (Welfare, Wealth and Work for Europe consortium) Working Paper No 56 – March 2014
[3] The Spirit Level – Richard G. Wilkinson and Kate Pickett – (2009) Allen Lane

inequality causing increased anxiety and illness, eroding trust and encouraging excessive consumption – are ignored by governments who may feel powerless to change things or who are overwhelmed by other priorities.

John Locke – described as the father of classical liberalism – thought of government as a social compact among people to which the institution of government is not a party, but rather a trust for the people, defined and limited "to the publick good of the Society"[4]. In the superb essay which opens this book, Nigel Dower examines and defines the thinking on "New Liberalism" which, he says, has at its heart the idea that liberty is about the public interest – "liberty and the conditions of liberty or of reasonable living for *everyone*." Liberalism now also normally comprises the idea that the full exercise of freedom requires also that key social rights are secured to everyone.

I am indebted to discussion with former Scottish Environment and Rural Affairs Minister Ross Finnie for an idea which we might call "Locke Plus" – that Locke's powerful concept of government as trust might be widened to include both the idea of intergenerational duties, which is currently much discussed, and the idea of a broader sustainability which encompasses not just the sustainability of natural resources but also the long term sustainability of our economy and our society.

In this context, poverty wages, whilst they may be "maintainable", are not "sustainable" – people cannot exist on them indefinitely, and society should not permit them indefinitely. In similar vein, company profits should be sustainable in the longer term within a system of economic checks and balances, rather than maintainable at the highest possible level (often involving either asset stripping, employment stripping or poverty wages).

---

[4] John Locke – Two Treatises of Government: Second Treatise (1689)

An aging population requires a sensible pensions policy based on long term considerations – and the major reforms introduced by Steve Webb as Liberal Democrat Pensions Minister in the Coalition government has given us this in significant measure. But, amongst the wielders of the greatest financial clout in the UK are the directors, trustees and senior executives of pension funds – our pension funds – who operate in a largely secret world whilst exercising the power given to them by our money on remuneration committees and in investment decisions which shape our economy.

Even in health, one of the central priorities for governments over many years, the core objective of improving wellbeing has sunk without trace under a welter of targets designed to determine how long you have to wait for the next stage of the treatment process.

All these things are perverse and point in entirely the wrong direction. Liberals, by contrast, are interested in the control of excess power in the general or public interest. Sustainability – Locke Plus – is the key to this and the essays in this book, whether expressly or implicitly, almost all look to put flesh on this general theme.

The death of capitalism?

The latter half of the twentieth century saw the death of Communism and also of Socialism. On a longer economic time frame, it may be that the banking crisis has also signalled the imminent death of Capitalism, at least in the sense we have known it, based on competition in a free market. Of course, such a market continues to exist at the bottom level. Shopkeepers, window cleaners, electricians, plumbers, hairdressers, restaurateurs and family solicitors continue to exist in a broadly free market. But the portion of the market available to them has shrunk as the supermarkets, the pubcos and the corporate lawyers take an increasing slice of income in the sector.

It is, though, difficult to describe the banking sector, the defence industry, the car industry, pharmaceuticals, the alcohol or food products industries, or the media in the same way. The commercial entities which dominate in some of these fields are either quasi monopolies or cartels – at the very least they operate on a global basis rather than at a national or regional level. The trenchant defence of the European Union and the European project mounted by Sir Graham Watson, until recently the UK's longest-serving Liberal Democrat MEP, should be read by anyone tempted by the seductive fallacies of UKIP – and, more so, by those who are not!

We are not yet at the stage where a latter day Adam Smith or Karl Marx synthesises a new and compelling description of post-free market, global capitalism – or of the alternatives to it. But I hope that these essays will play a small part in killing the idea that there is no alternative to the greed, the exorbitant and unaccountable power, the potential for economic collapse, the insecurity, exploitation and poverty wages which seem to be key downsides of the way in which things work at present. The essay drawn from Prateek Buch's sustained critique of the policies of austerity casts a number of interesting insights into this.

The Little Yellow Book and the Coalition
This book follows on the success of The Little Yellow Book[5] which we published 2 years ago in the aftermath of the electoral disasters sustained by the Liberal Democrats at the Scottish Parliament, Welsh Assembly and English Council elections of the previous year, largely as a consequence of the Coalition and our participation in it.

Nick Clegg led the Liberal Democrats into the Coalition government in 2010 following an indecisive general election;

---

[5] *The Little Yellow Book* – ed. Robert Brown and Nigel Lindsay - Liberal Futures March 2012

a major cause of the indecisive result and a major rationale for the Coalition was the pressing need to clear up the aftermath of the banking meltdown – which, whatever else, had not been caused or contributed to by the Liberal Democrats, or indeed by the Conservatives. David Steel, in a memorable phrase, described the Coalition as a "business arrangement born out of necessity". And so it was, in the eyes of many of us who supported the Coalition at its inception and later. Instead, the Party leadership, endorsed by the Special Conference, agreed a full blown coalition covering the whole gamut of government.

It is not the purpose of this collection of essays to render a final judgement on that decision, nor on the successes and failures of the Coalition, the high points and the low points of its policies, or how far the cause of Liberalism was advanced by the Party's participation in the Government. This is the job of historians and will need the perspective of time. Some excellent comparative reflexions on the Coalition come from the diverse contributions of the distinguished Liberal blogger Caron Lindsay, from journalist and historian Willis Pickard, from my co-editor Nigel Lindsay, and from former Scottish Minister Ross Finnie.

Our purpose is rather to provide some perspectives on the last four years, to test performance against both Liberal objectives and in how far the underlying political challenges have been met. More than that, however, we want to build on the success of *The Little Yellow Book* in developing a narrative for Liberalism going forward – a "Liberalism of the People" as I have described it previously.

It has to be recognised too that the Liberal Democrat Party itself is seen by much of the public as part of the political establishment and part of the problem of alienation and distrust that undermines our democracy. Our belief is that the Party, whether in government or not, has to rediscover a narrative and a politics which is anti-establishment, which is robustly critical of abuse and excess of power wherever it occurs, which aims to represent the general interest of the public and which sides with those who lack power in our society.

Part of the way forward is to strive for the more sustainable economy and society identified by Ross Finnie as key to the future health of our country. This means amongst other things that neither the natural resources of the planet nor the interests and well being of future generations can be sacrificed or laid waste by the present generation – the new issue of inter-generational justice.

It is time too to end the tyranny of spin doctors and focus groups. As Russell Johnston once commented: 'Democracy cannot flourish on a diet of triviality'

It is the job of political movements to provide a political analysis of the challenges of the day and to offer a direction of travel which will deal with them. In the case of the Liberal Democrats, this means a programme which offers hope and opportunity, enhances freedom and life chances (a broad conception of positive, enabling freedoms such as the Beveridge freedoms from squalor, ignorance, want, idleness and disease), supports the general interest against excessive corporate power or monopoly, and which aims to raise the quality and integrity of our democracy.

Issues in the Book
In these pages are some important ideas and directions of travel:

- The concept of political and economic sustainability, to give body to the mandate of the state to hold public power on behalf of, and as trustee for, the people.

- A new federal conception, not just of the future of the United Kingdom in the aftermath of the Scottish referendum, but of the way in which our political life is organised and understood – a pluralist, diverse and rich variety of peoples and cultures but rooted in the traditional sense of freedom and the rule of law that has been the specific contribution on our country to the world.

- Whether the austerity programme pursued by the Coalition and which essentially followed the Labour government's strategy as laid down by Alastair Darling achieved its purpose – and more importantly whether there is scope for modifying the strategy against the background of the improving economy – to raise living standards or to provide more resource for example to pressured key services.

- Whether the reconstruction of the economy has laid a sustainable basis for tackling its shortcomings and avoiding future disasters.

- The need for true welfare reform, righting the balance between the state and the employer so that employees are paid proper wages for their labour, rather than having poverty wages subsided by the state under some latter day Speenhamland system –developed by Robert Aldridge in his important essay.

- The need to rebalance the nation, to meet the challenge of London (Tony Hughes), to support the more human scale values of the Highlands and Islands of Scotland which have, as Kate Stephen reminds us, succoured Liberals and the Liberal Party over so many generations, perhaps to build and let flourish the "City States" within our country spoken of by David Steel

- The central importance of human rights as a framework and test of our values, both at home and abroad, spelling out what respect for other human beings and their freedoms truly means

- The ugliness and moral decay of an economic system that tends both to widen the gap between rich and poor –

and to justify it by the core Liberal value of freedom, as if freedom adhered to and was the right of markets, corporations and global institutions rather than of people.

- The deficiencies of globalism that raise questions about the adequacy of our view of the market economy, which now seems rather cartelised on a world scale, incapable of being controlled by national governments if at all, and a major cause of inequality, injustice and oppression in the world.

The years since 2010 when the Party entered the Coalition government in the aftermath of the banking collapse are likely to be a time and an experience seared into the soul of Liberal Democrats for generations to come. An honest appraisal of that venture is vital for the health of our cause, rather as doctors prescribed the drawing of blood by leeches to relieve illness in days gone by. Indeed some might say that the Coalition experience itself was rather like that!

Liberal Democracy is of course a political philosophy but it is also an attitude to life, a view, as Locke had it, that democratic representation is a position of trusteeship for the people and, as we might now argue, for the planet and for future generations. It is also a challenge to strive endlessly so that, as Russell Johnston put it, "man" might have life and have it abundantly.

These essays, some by Party members and some by contributors outside it, are, in their various ways, an attempt to develop the original aim laid down in *The Little Yellow Book*, of articulating a modern Liberalism of the people, fit for the modern age which will serve to widen the ground on which we stand in the difficult days that will follow the current Coalition. We hope our book will help to re inspire a new generation of Liberals with a sense of the depth, vitality and necessity – the magic even – of our cause, which should be endlessly challenging and endlessly restless to give opportunity and wide freedom to our people.

Liberalism

Nigel Dower

Introduction

In the chapter I defend a version of liberalism which is similar to the 'new liberalism' of the early twentieth century of T. H. Green and L. T. Hobhouse, sometimes called social liberalism, liberal socialism or welfare liberalism. It also owes a lot to the ideas of two more modern 'liberal' thinkers, namely John Rawls and Amartya Sen. As such it is in broad contrast to the old or classical liberalism of the 19th Century which stressed laissez faire and the minimal state, and also to a modern influential version of liberalism called libertarianism or neo-liberalism which in some respects harks back to the earlier classical liberalism. The guiding question for me is: what makes liberty valuable? The answer put simply is that whilst it is good to have liberty in the sense of not being prevented from doing certain things, what makes it really valuable is one being able to exercise one's liberty or exercise it properly; that is, it is in large measure valuable if the conditions are in place for the effective exercise of liberty. For instance, it is one thing to have free speech (e.g. there is no law preventing one from speaking one's mind), it is another to be able to exercise it articulately because one has had a reasonable education. It is one thing to be free to pursue whatever hobbies one wants to (e.g. public opinion or social conventions do not make it difficult), it is another to have sufficient resources to be able to pursue interesting hobbies. For these conditions to exist for everyone in society, many things need to be in place – certain political and legal institutions, the provision of education, access to health care and various forms of social protection. For these to be in place there needs to be a general commitment to social justice. Furthermore, in the modern world, if this conception of liberalism is accepted, it has serious implications for any society in the rest of the world and also to future generations who will need the conditions of liberty in place for them too. The idea of liberalism as 'social liberalism' does not strictly entail it, but in fact, I shall argue later in the chapter, liberalism needs to be cosmopolitan and committed to sustainability.

What follows is largely a personal exploration of what liberalism means to me today: it does not pretend to be an authoritative analysis of what diffferent liberals today may say, let alone map onto actual Libdem policies.

The worth of liberty

To get to the the heart of my main point, let me contrast the approach of John Rawls in *A Theory of Justice* (1971) with that of Robert Nozick in *Anarchy, State and Utopia* (1974) who advocated libertarianism as a contrast to Rawls' idea of social justice (Rawls 1971; Nozick 1974). John Rawls and Robert Nozick were American philosophers who were trying to articulate the social values that underlay a modern society such as the USA (but which they both thought were applicable universally). Rawls' book was monumental both in size (it was some 600 pages long) and in impact, not just amongst philosophers but also amongst sociologists, political theorists, legal theorists and international relations theorists. He felt the need to articulate an essentially liberal approach in the face of a then much more worked out socialist/Marxist critique. What surprised him was that the main reaction came from the other side of the political spectrum, and one of the key figures in this reaction was Robert Nozick: basically Rawls' view of liberalism was not a pure enough version which was libertarianism. Although there has been much water under the bridge since then in terms of the debate about what makes a society liberal, I feel that what Rawls and Nozick said still sums up a key fault line. My engagement with political philosophy was really triggered by teaching this material, so that is why I am using them in what follows.

Rawls argued for two principles that should underline the structure of a just society: the equal liberty principle and the difference principle. The equal liberty principle was that that everyone should have as much liberty as was consistent with others having the like liberty. The difference principle was about justified differences of wealth and status: basically inequalities are only justified if they lead to the worst off group being better off that under any other arrangement (because such differences contribute to the general well being of all). The latter idea has proved controversial because it is too strong a demand of justice, but the underlying thought behind it is valid. Rawls thinks that the intuition behind justice is that, were we not to know our position in society or about our abilities and attitudes (the 'veil of ignorance' condition), we would want to ensure that we had both freedom and a reasonable material basis for living (i.e. we were not too poor). In fact the two ideas are linked by another important aspect of Rawls' account: he stresses the equal *worth* of liberty. We need for instance sufficient wealth, education etc. to make the exercise of liberty effective. We also need not merely laws that allow us various freedoms (movement, assembly, religion etc.) but also an effective legal framework in which laws are complied with and enforced, so that we can exercise our liberties without fear or hindrance. A necessary condition of this is that there are effective restrictions on how liberty is exercised (e.g. in labour laws and, we would now stress, environmental laws) and that there is progressive taxation e.g. to finance education and reasonable access to healthcare. One of the ways of bringing this out is through the distinction between fair equality of opportunity and formal equality of opportunity. A society might have formal equality of opportunity if jobs and public offices are open to people from whatever backgrounds, but this could be consistent with large numbers of people because of poverty or lack of education being unable to take advantage of these formal opportunities, whereas fair equality of opportunity requires that everyone has a reasonable level of wealth and education. (This is easier said than done but at least the conception of a fully just society is one in which this ideal is achieved.)

Nozick's response to Rawls was to argue that the right to liberty, especially economic liberty, is central and to reject Rawls' idea of distributive justice as represented by the difference principle and by implication the importance of the worth of liberty as being central to its value. The right to liberty is just that, the right to as much freedom to act as one chooses, with a 'minimal state' acting as a nightwatchman to maintain the rule of law, external defence and providing such public goods as are essential for everyone. Liberty for Nozick acts as a 'side-constraint' on what may be done to limit that liberty, it is not a goal that the state pursues (which he criticizes as an example of a 'rights maximisation' model). In the sphere of economic activity, what makes a transaction just is the process involved: a contract e.g. of employment or transfer of goods is just if it observes two conditions, that of non-coercion and that of non-deception. If the repeated exercise of just transactions leads to very unequal outcomes including extreme poverty, there is nothing unjust in this. Nozick's 'entitlement' theory is an example of what he calls a historical account because it looks at the the history of the transactions; it is contrasted with what he calls patterned accounts (e.g. distribution according to merit) or end-state accounts (e.g. a just society is one in which there is a certain distribution of wealth). For him progressive taxation in which much more money is taken from the rich to finance services and support for the poor/disadvantaged is in effect theft from the rich because it is a denial of part of their economic freedom.

This position of Nozick's may be rather strong even for liberals who are more drawn to the libertarian model, but the contrast with Rawls brings out a kind of fault line in liberal thought. Are we trying to create a society in which everyone has the conditions in which their liberty has a value and worth – which requires much more than a minimal state – or are we trying to create or maintain a society in which everyone is minimally restricted by law to do their own thing, even if this results in many people having a liberty which is worth very little because they are so poor, uneducated or otherwise disadvantaged? To put it another way, is a liberally just society one in which there is, inter alia, an overall fair distribution of life opportunities, or one in which what makes a society just is the summation of lots of individual transactions between individuals that happen to meet formal requirements of things like non-deception and non-coercion? (These things are by the way very important: it is their adequacy I am questioning.)

The capabilities approach

So the crucial distinction is I am suggesting between promoting freedom as a formal set of limits on others and the state, and promoting freedom as promoting the conditions which enable freedoms to be exercised effectively. This is very much the theme of a modern influential economist/philosopher Amartya Sen, who along with a number of others such as Martha Nussbaum, promotes the 'capabilities approach' (Sen 1999; Nussbaum 2000). Sen's main concern is with an adequate account of development, which he sees as multi-dimensional and not just about economic growth. His account is relevant not only for poorer countries but for richer countries like the UK. He characterizes development 'as the process of expanding the real freedoms that people enjoy', and sees it as providing the conditions in which all people are able first to develop a full range of capabilities (requiring proper nutrition, nurture and education) and then exercising these capabilities in 'functionings' (through a generally strong rights framework, access to work, medical aid and other forms of support) in lives which they have 'reason to value'. For me this is a deeply 'liberal' conception of society and what real development is about.

Two further contrasts are worth mentioning that help to bring out the difference between the new liberalism I am broadly supporting and the more libertarian vision.

Social embeddedness

It is feature of some liberal thought – often seen as the key problem of liberalism for its critics – that liberalism involves a conception of the individual as an 'isolated rational chooser' rather than as 'flesh and blood' people embedded in social relations. Sometimes, how fairly I am not sure, the thought of Immanuel Kant is invoked here given his account of moral autonomy. Liberalism is sometimes contrasted with communitarianism that stresses that people's identities are shaped by community relations and shared traditions. However there is nothing in the new liberalism as such to entail commitment to a rugged individualism that sees individuals as isolated units with minimal ties and responsibilities towards others in society, and much in it to reject it. This idea of rugged individualism is more congenial to those who espouse a more libertarian view of the individual whose main duty in response to others generally (apart from family and personal relations) is simply not to harm other people (a negative duty or minimal morality conception). The new liberalism is entirely consistent with seeing and indeed for many new liberals essentially involves seeing individuals as embedded in social relations – from family units, through local community to wider socially cohesive society with significant positive duties and responsibilities to promote justice and indeed the conditions of liberty, as I have suggested above, within that society and beyond. To achieve formal liberty all we need do is refrain for interfering; to achieve the worth of liberty requires active engagement. It does not just happen. The importance of communal relations at all levels is both intrinsic and instrumental; that is, our well-being is constituted by 'freedom in relations' or what Merleau-Ponty called 'situated freedom', but also communal relations help make people more likely to contribute to the general interest or public good. Another way of marking the distinction between the new liberalism and libertarianism precisely turns on this point that the new liberalism is about the public interest in the sense that it is liberty and the conditions of liberty or of reasonable living for *everyone* that is the object of concern. By contrast for the libertarian the right to liberty is a side-constraint, as I noted earlier, on what the state can do which is merely to allow as much of it as possible: there is no goal of *promoting* the public interest or common good (or if there is, it is in a much weaker sense).

The importance of other values

A further contrast has to do with how we understand the value of liberty and whether we see it as the value above all else. Is what is important that we have liberty or rather a range of liberties to do or not do certain things and so long as the state or others in society do not stop me from exercising my liberty (except where justified if my exercise invades another's liberty), then that is all that matters? To be sure, it is central to all liberalism to say that both the possession of liberty and the exercise of liberty are important. The possession of liberty involves not merely an objective social reality in which certain things (e.g. religious practice; free speech) are indeed permitted and protected but also the subjective awareness of this, and so a person can when he chooses exercise that liberty in confidence that he will not be stopped or interfered with.

Bu the social liberalism which I am supporting goes much further than this. Apart from stressing what I have already mentioned, that what makes the possession of liberty valuable is the knowledge that one has the resources – financial, educational etc. – or the capabilities to exercise it effectively and what make the exercise of it more likely is the awareness that one can do so and do so effectively, there are two things to mention. First, liberty is partly valuable because it leads to the development of the person. This was a key idea in an early liberal thinker namely John Stuart Mill; here liberty is not merely an end in itself but a means by which a person could develop her full potential as a unique individual, or as we might say now pursue her own authentic life-journey (or as Sen would say exercise a full range of capabilities in a full or rounded life). The point here is that whilst liberty is clearly central to this possibility, the value of a full life is not exhausted in terms of liberty. What makes a life go well is not merely having and exercising liberties but many other things.

This is an aspect of a more general point. If having and exercising liberties is not merely a good in itself but also a means to something else of value, we have to ask what other things are of value. Of course one could argue that having liberty or freedom is good as a means to the further enjoyment of them later or to other liberties and freedoms, but this would I think be a very restrictive view of what human well being consists in. Personal relationships and friendships, interesting work and hobbies and various kinds of enjoyment, the pursuit of knowledge, quite apart from basics such as not starving, being healthy and being secure, are all dimensions of a good human life, and they are all good in themselves however much or otherwise our enjoyment of them is linked to the exercise of our liberties. If we as liberals stress liberty, it is not merely because it is important in its own right but because of its crucial instrumental role in making the enjoyment of all these other goods more likely.

Once it is acknowledged that liberty is valuable not merely in its own right but as a means to many other goods, we can also readily see that these goods are goods for other people as well as oneself, including their liberites as well. To be sure the main point here is that my liberty is valuable to me because its exercise leads me to enjoy or have many other things. But we can and should be in favour of liberty because it also leads (at least generally) to other people achieving well-being in various ways. Part of the ethical value of having (effective) liberty is that it contributes to well-being generally. (For the libertarian liberal it is just this way of understanding the value of liberty that is questioned – hence Nozick's key point about the right to liberty being a side-constraint. See my comment above about the public interest.) Much of our concern for the environment for instance is premised on trying not to undermine the life conditions of people anywhere and in the future which are thought to be threatened by environmental degradation and resource scarcity which will put in question access to things like enough food, water and other basic goods. It is these goods that are the focus of attention rather than liberties themselves.

If one goes a step further and recognises that nonhuman life has a value (or even just the sentient lives of higher animals), then our policies, insofar as they recognise the need to protect the life conditions of these living things, explicitly reflect values other than liberty values. These are not of course values which I enjoy, let alone values I enjoy because I exercise liberty, but like the human well-being of other humans I may recognise I have *inter alia* a duty to promote (or at least not undermine) them. Of course not all social liberals would acknowledge that non-human living things have any intrinsic value (merely a use value to human beings) – it is not part of what liberalism means – but there is certainly nothing inconsistent for a liberal to acknowledge such a value. Whether or not one recognises this, the more general point I am making which I think is implicit in the social liberal position (which may be absent from the libertarian position that makes liberty itself *the* value) is that the importance of liberty rests partly on providing much of the enabling conditions for other human values – in oneself as well as in others – to be realised as well.

Further contrasts

So far I have tried to map out what I see as the main features of an approach to liberalism which may be called the new liberalism or social liberalism, and I have contrasted it to the libertarian model. I am not claiming that all liberals fall neatly into one or other camp or that these are clear-cut polarities. Many individual liberal thinkers may wish to combine elements of both.

What I want to do now is pick out five areas of thought in which liberals might take somewhat different positions. These different positions may all be taken within the broad perspective of new liberalism: they are not as such points of difference between new liberals and libertarianism or classical liberalism. They concern political liberty, multiculturalism, freedom of thought, global implications and the environment. I shall deal with the first three briefly but say more about the latter two because they are of particular importance in the modern world.

Political liberty

T. H. Marshall once argued that there are three types of rights of citizens in a state: political rights or rights to political participation, civil rights or the rights to non-interference by the state or others in such areas as freedom of thought, religion, assembly and freedom from arbitrary attack, discrimination or lack of due process, and socio-economic rights or the rights to receive various kinds of benefit, such education, health care, pensions or unemployment benefits (Marshall 1973). Classical liberalism tended to focus on civil liberties/rights in contrast to the so-called 'liberty of the ancients' which was the freedom to participate in 'res publica' of one's state. The new liberalism I have been giving a version of very much takes to heart Marshall's third category of rights namely social and economic rights, partly, as we have seen, because it is a bedrock of the effective exercise of civil rights. But liberalism, classical or new, does not, conceptually, make a lot of the possession and exercise of political liberty. Of course liberals have broadly been supportive of democracy, namely that citizens should have the right to choose governments in elections, and as a political party it has long been a party of active members or party activists, but the question is: how much emphasis is put on political participation in democratic processes as something important for citizens in general?

Curiously enough some thinkers actually contrast what they see as the republican conception as opposed to the liberal conception of citizenship (see e.g. Miller 1999). The republican conception is about citizens as actively engaged in res publica ('public things' or the public space in which Habermas saw public deliberation taking place) – not just every five years but all the time. This is important both because such active participation is crucial to a properly functioning democracy but also because such participation is actually an important part of what makes us fully human (the point that Aristotle was making when he said the 'man is a social animal'). By contrast the so-called 'liberal' conception is of citizens who enjoy a whole range of rights or liberties to pursue their own conceptions of the good as they choose: whether or not they see active political engagement as part of that is accidental. Maybe this conception of the liberties that are at the heart of liberalism is attractive to some liberals, but my thought is that actually the possession and and exercise of political liberty is an important part of what liberalism should mean today. This is not merely because I believe that participation in the affairs of one's society is an important part of a fully human life (it gives us some sense of being marginally in control of our destiny) but because if we want the kind of society in which the other two types of rights are realised and the worth of liberty is generally secured, a vibrant society of politically active citizens is actually an important part of what is needed.

Multiculturalism

How should a liberal respond to the fact that in many modern pluralist societies such as the UK there are many different groups with different ethinic and cultural backgrounds and, often going alongside this, different faiths? Here liberals are caught in a dilemma, because on the one hand we want to espouse the freedom of groups to follow their way of life, and on the other hand the liberal conception has historically centred on the primacy of the individual, on individual rights and on a secular basis for the promotion and protection of liberties, though of course not being opposed to religious perspective of many individuals: the liberal conception is neutral between those who have religious faith and those who have none. The trouble is that many groups are groups whose worldviews reject precisely these things in favour of a more communal conception of well-being and rooted in some religious faith. If liberalism sticks to its radical individualism then it can at best adopt a pragmatic accommodation to groups with different perspectives. On the other hand it is possible for liberals to adopt a somewhat more generous approach by recognising that whilst liberty does indeed focus on that of individuals, it can extend to include the liberty of groups, and can, beyond mere toleration embrace multiculturalism and positive interfaith relations.

John Rawls in his later book *Political Liberalism* actually grapples with this: whereas in his earlier work he was primarily concerned with ensuring the liberty of individuals to pursue 'their conceptions of the good', he later recognised that in modern complex societies there are different 'comprehensive visions' of different groups, and what we need is a political conception of justice that acknowledges what he calls an 'overlapping consensus', which each comprehensive vision can support for its own reasons (Rawls 1993). This is however an immensely complicated issue I do not pretend to address properly. Clearly there are limits to what one may welcome, for instance if groups actually advocate a rejection of the liberal democratic order they are part of, or of course think that terrorism is a legitimate way of challenging the state and what it stands for. All I am saying is that a liberalism that is relevant to the 21st century needs to be somewhat accommodating to what may be called the liberty of groups as well as the liberty of individuals.

The value of freedom of thought

Another issue which may divide modern liberals of the 'new liberalism' approach is over why freedom of thought is valuable. Here I am sympathetic to an older view, one clearly articulated by John Stuart Mill, that one of the main reasons to champion freedom of thought and expression, apart from the value of people having their intellectual or spiritual journeys and thus achieving their own development, is that the 'truth' is more likely to emerge through the free and uninhibited exchange of ideas and arguments. This contrasts with a typically modern view that some liberals may have, along with thinkers of other political persuasions as well, that there is no truth to be had in many areas. Thus some form of relativism is held that there are no right or wrong views in areas such as ethics, political values, aesthetics or religious beliefs. (A stronger relativist or postmodern view might hold this also for scientific 'knowledge' in particular and factual 'knowledge' in general.). I am myself sympathetic to the older view that however difficult it is to reach reasonable views in these areas, the search for moral and religious 'truth' or at least more rationally grounded positions and arguments is a valid one, and that open debate and discussion is the best basis for trying to achieve this. If one abandons this in favour of relativism, one has no principled basis for rejecting extremist views (since they are no worse than other views). One also deprives oneself as we will see later of a principled basis for criticising the behaviour of other countries in international relations.

This position may seem to be at odds with my advocating embracing multiculturalism above, because it may seem as though I am saying that one has to accept the variety of different religious faith positions. But the tension is only apparent not real. Apart from of course the immense practical importance of good relations between different groups, the emphasis upon dialogue and positive exchanges of views rather than argumentative confrontation is more likely to conduce to truth and indeed to the recognition that each group may have some measure of access to the truth: in religious matters it seems unlikely that one group will have the monopoly of truth anyway.

International relations

The liberalism that I am advocating is one that is firmly rooted in the recognition that if liberty is valuable for the reasons I have argued inside a country like the UK, it is valuable anywhere in the world, and that, other things being equal, we have commitments to promote and certainly not to impede the realization of liberty elsewhere. Given the analysis I have given of the worth of liberty and of how the conditions of liberty are necessary which include *inter alia* the basic goods of life – food, water, health, economic well-being – the argument for the universal value of liberty looks much less like an appeal to specifically western values and more like an argument for the conditions of life that are needed anywhere in the world, whatever the differences in culture and so on. In any case if as I have argued liberalism includes the acceptance of other values as well, these other values are certainly universally applicable. So what I am advocating is a version of liberalism which is sometimes called liberal internationalism, but which I prefer to call liberal cosmopolitanism.

I am 'advocating' this version of liberalism because I am well aware that this account is not strictly entailed by the basic position of social liberalism. It is perfectly possible for someone to be social liberal and not accept the global approach I have outlined. That is, one could be a liberal nationalist or even a liberal communitarian. One might hold that although liberty is indeed valid elsewhere in the world, it is the task of each political community to promote and protect liberal values and other values within each political community, and maybe cooperate with other like-minded communities in certain respects. (Indeed this view is somewhat similar to that advocated by John Rawls in his last major work *The Laws of Peoples* (Rawls 1999); whereas I think he hit on some important truths in his earlier writings, he is not as I see it right on this issue). Or one could adopt the relativist view (I mentioned earlier) and say that whilst within certain political communities (such as the UK) these values are indeed the ones accepted or appropriate given our shared traditions, they simply aren't appropriate to other political communities with other traditions.

So why should we accept a broadly universal value framework and the idea of trans-boundary obligations to promote and not to impede human well-being anywhere?

Let me back up a little here and offer an account of cosmopolitanism. Thomas Pogge, who effectively offers a liberal cosmopolitan analysis in his influential book *World*

Poverty and Human Rights, offers the following general definition:

'Three elements are shared by all cosmopolitan positions. First, individualism: the ultimate units of concern are human beings, or persons – rather than, say, family lines, tribes, ethnic, cultural or religious communities, nations, or states. ... Second, universality: the status of ultimate unit of concern attaches to every living human being equally – not merely to some sub-set, such as men, aristocrats, Aryans, whites, or Muslims. Third, generality: this special status has global force. Persons are ultimate units of concern for everyone – not only for their compatriots, fellow religionists, or suchlike.' (Pogge 2002: 169)

What makes people ultimate units of concern is that they are trying to achieve their well-being and this well-being involves as we have seen earlier not merely basic goods such as food, water, health, shelter but the conditions of a reasonable livelihood in which they are able to make effective choices. As Henry Shue argues, there are three basic rights to subsistence, security and basic liberty (Shue 1996). Now whilst it is clear that not all societies in the world espouse the full account of liberties as advocated by liberals, there is a universal concern about the conditions of effective agency and control over one's life. That is, almost all people – ordinary people – will have this concern, whatever the prevailing political conditions are – oppressive, authoritarian, tyrannical and so on. If liberalism, as I have earlier argued, is about respecting ways of life that are not typically how self-styled liberals wish to live, then in acknowledging these, the liberal can acknowledge the universal value of agency, even if she is vigorously opposed to many forms of political regime that deny human rights and often undermine not only the liberties that liberals hold dear but the conditions of effective agency as well. But that apart, it is important to recognize that the conditions for the effective exercise of liberties as understood by liberals are in large measure *the same conditions* needed for the effective realization of ways of life that are not characterized in liberal terms, then we can recognize that the basic conditions of human well-being are in many respects the same all over the world. Since it is well recognised that in many parts of the world vast numbers of people live in conditions that do not equate with conditions for a reasonable and full life, the recognition of trans-boundary obligations or what Pogge calls global force is surely reasonable.

Why should we accept these transboundary obligations? First let me take positive obligations to assist with development through aid. One should arguably accept a conception of ethics which is 'open' in the sense that wherever we have the capacity to affect the lives of others – however distant – then in principle we should be willing, to respond where it is appropriate to do so. That is, such transboundary action is an aspect of the altruistic or Good Samaritan dimension to ethics. But even if one did not accept this as an application of the altruistic aspect of ethics, there are two further reasons that particularly apply in the modern world. First, it may be in our collective interests to ensure that people achieve well-being anywhere in the world, at one level to reduce the likelihood of conflict, at another level to encourage mutually beneficial relations in the future such as trading relations. Second, given that the world is so inter-connected now through economic and other forms of globalization, there is a sense in which we in countries in the North have benefitted so much from this, that we owe it to others who have benefitted less to do something.

But our obligations do not merely arise in respect of obligations to give aid. Perhaps more significant is the challenge of ensuring that our general trading policies and those of large companies that operate from the North and bring large profits back to Northern countries, do not actually harm people elsewhere or in various ways impede development.   This claim, one that for instance Pogge is interested in making, is of course somewhat controversial, but I will merely add a few thoughts which are the tip of a large iceberg. The idea that our trading processes might not be all that good for people in poorer countries is implicitly acknowledged by the increasing interest in the UK, not least liberals and liberally minded people, in fair trade. If we prefer to buy Fairtrade bananas, tea, coffee and now a whole host of other things too, it is because we implicitly acknowledge (if not explicitly assert) that bananas etc. bought otherwise come through economic relations which are not (as) fair or just. Apart from the general issue of whether the terms of trade are often sufficiently favorable to poorer counties, there are specific issues of concern such as the way the whole intellectual property right regime (TRIPS), presided over by the WTO, seems to trap poor farmers in situations in which big companies do rather well and they don't. There is also the whole issue of tax havens which, as things currently stand, enable big companies to avoid paying much tax in poor countries or indeed elsewhere. Insofar as we in rich countries accept that this is how the world economy works and indeed are both beneficiaries of this and to some extent participants in this, then we have some responsibility to think of how we can reduce our dependence on processes such as these, both as individuals and as citizens of a country whose policies are in in our hands.

There are of course other dimensions to global responsibility as well. Apart from a commitment to aid (development assistance as well as emergency assistance) and global economic justice, there is a commitment to other things like environmental sustainability, peace-building (including I would argue reducing our dependence on the arms trade), promotion of international law including human rights law, strengthening the United Nations, and having relatively open borders. In all these respects, a commitment to liberalism ought to be commitment to taking the global dimension seriously.

The environment

One area where arguably we are all collectively involved in contributing to harm is indeed our contribution to climate change. Few doubt that if we collectively continue in our carbon profligate ways, we will be storing up serious trouble for people living in the future, maybe ourselves and children, certainly our grandchildren and generations after that. Some would argue that climate change is already happening in many parts of the world, and that the negative effects are already being felt in parts of Africa for instance where the people have made a minimal contribution to the problems (and so issues of compensation and assistance with adaptations arise too). Apart from climate change, pressures on the environment are occurring in many other ways as well, largely due to the relentless drive for development, particularly development as economic growth. Land degradation, depleted fish stocks and species loss are amongst the negative effects. In my own opinion, unless we tackle the obsession with economic growth, as well as finding all the technical solutions we can, the prospects for the future are not great. However, I am not going to say more about my own perspective but rather finish with some more general observations about sustainability and why in principle we need to be committed to sustainability. If we accept the principle, it is then up to each of us to work out what needs to be done to achieve it, and how large the changes are that are needed.

There is nothing good about sustainability itself. It all depends on what we want to sustain. If the Mafia wish to sustain their control of a city, we do not approve of either the goal or the means involved. If a very rich person wished to sustain his carbon intensive lifestyle (and was right in thinking he could do this), we would not commend it, because we would feel he has not asked the obvious universalizability question 'could everyone do this?' so we have to decide what things ought be sustained. Most people would recoil from the idea that all we need be concerned with is sustaining the conditions for a reasonable life for those living in our own country now. Why? Because we recognize that future generations have a right to reasonable conditions of life insofar as it is possible for us to enable them to have these, and because we recognize that people in other countries also have a right to reasonable conditions of life. If we put these two thoughts together , the answer is that whatever we do, it should as far as possible be consistent with enabling all people present and future to achieve the conditions of a reasonable life. (If we acknowledge as I said earlier that non-human life has a value, then that needs to be factored in too! But I put that aside here.)

If people elsewhere matter (cosmopolitanism) and future generations matter, then sustaining reasonable life conditions for all present and future is the very least that sustainability is all about. This goal is I believe achievable (just). To restrict our concern to our own country or to time present is morally partial and arbitrary. On the other hand, whilst clearly some growth is needed particularly in respect to the least well-off, the goal of universal economic growth for all present and future is I believe quite unrealistic. (It is a commitment to what Herman Daly called 'the impossibility theorem'.) There needs to be a paradigm shift in the way we think of what human well-being consists in. This is another big topic, though it is worth adding that the capabilities approach of Sen and others by focusing on the many dimensions of human well-being over and above economic well-being is a useful way into this re-evaluation.

My account of the scope of sustainability and what it entails is not self-evident from the point of view of a liberal or indeed a social liberal. There could be two sources of resistance. First, a liberal may not be cosmopolitan, as I indicated in the previous section, and thus have reservations about the extent of our obligations to people elsewhere in the world. Or he might have theoretical reservations about whether the current generation can have obligations to future generations who do not yet exist (there is quite a philosophical literature about such scepticism and there is no reason why a liberal might not be persuaded by this!). My earlier arguments about open morality extending as far as our capacity for effective agency extends applies in both cases. And if there was ever a case of collective self-interest requiring urgent collective action, the case of climate change is it. The argument that future generations don't exist and we don't know who they will be seems irrelevant if one considers that one day they will exist and when they exist they will have their well-being, needs and rights. That seems to make them relevant objects of our concern if what we do can affect them. (The fact that they cannot reciprocate seems irrelevant since reciprocity is not the only or even main basis for ethical relations.)

Most likely a liberal will not be tempted by these two lines of thought. However she might well accept the scope of sustainability (everyone present and future) but be much more optimistic about the possibility of business, development or life conceptions as usual, and so propose less radical solutions to our environmental problems. Here our differences are not ethical or theoretical but based on significantly different empirical or factual readings of our environmental situation (perhaps she is even a climate sceptic!). If so the discussion has to move into a scientific investigation into the facts of the matter (where one hopes that open debate will, as Mill noted, lead to the truth on these matters). All that remains for me to say, as an ethical theorist interested in liberalism, is this: whatever the liberal's 'take' on the empirical facts about our environment, the main thing is the moral commitment to sustainability as I have outlined it, and then to asking in the light of that commitment 'what can I advocate that I honestly believe is achievable?'.

Conclusion

I have outlined an approach to liberalism in the tradition of new/social liberalism which stresses both that for liberty to have its full value, background conditions need to be in place which enable the effective exercise of liberty, and these background conditions require more than the minimal state and things such as progressive taxation to fund education, free health service and so on. It also acknowledges that liberty is not merely an end in itself but a means to the realization of a range of other human goods. It also recognizes that as individuals in society we have obligations to provide the conditions of liberty; we are not isolated individuals whose rights to liberty act as side-constraints to what others may do. To this basic conception of social liberalism I have added a number of further aspects which whilst not strictly entailed by social liberalism, are reasonable additions. First, a commitment to political liberty as an expression of active citizenship. Second, a commitment to multiculturalism and a recognition of the right/liberty of groups as well as of individuals. Third, a recognition of the importance of freedom of thought residing in the greater likelihood of truth emerging rather than in the claim that there is no truth to emerge (relativism). Fourth, an understanding of liberalism as cosmopolitan both in regard to a broadly universal idea of agency and choice as valuable and in regard to trans-boundary obligations both to support and not undermine human well-being elsewhere. Fifth, an account of sustainability as a commitment to doing what we can to enable all people present and future to enjoy the conditions of a reasonable life. No modest task but this is what we owe to our fellow human beings.

Bibliography

Marshall, T. H. (1973). *Class, Citizenship and Social Development*. Westport CN: Greenwood Press.

Miller, D. (1999). 'Bounded citizenship'. In K. Hutchings & R. Dannreuther (eds) (1999). *Cosmopolitan Citizenship*. Basingstoke: Macmillan.

Nussbaum, M. C. (2000). *Women and Human Development: The Capabilities Approach*. Cambridge, UK: Cambridge University Press.

Pogge, Th. (2002). *World Poverty and Human Rights*. Cambridge: Cambridge University Press.

Rawls, J. (1971). *A Theory of Justice*. Cambridge MA: Harvard University Press,

Rawls, J. (1993). *Political Liberalism*. New York: Columbia University Press.

Rawls, J. (1999). *The Law of Peoples*. Cambridge MA: Harvard University Press.

Sen. A. (1999). *Development as Freedom*. Oxford: Oxford University Press.

Shue, H. (1996). *Basic Rights: Subsistence, Affluence, and U.S. Foreign Policy*. Princeton, N.J.: Princeton University Press.

The Financial Crash
and its Aftermath

Economic Prosperity for all at a time of austerity

Prateek Buch (with Robert Brown)

As I write this, the media is full of upbeat statements about how the recovery is in full swing, GDP is higher than before the recession, a million new jobs have been created in the private sector, and the deficit is on track to be eliminated by 2017–18. Indeed the UK economy is growing at the fastest rate of any of the G7 economies. Most of the headlines come from the Chancellor and other Conservative Ministers with the occasional plea that none of this would have happened without the Liberal Democrats providing stable and secure government (and indeed cushioning the effects of the recession on the less well off by the tax changes and other measures).

It is certainly true that the raw measures of the state of the economy are showing signs of a return to "normality". But major and important questions remain: was the government's austere response to the crisis correct? Was recovery enhanced or delayed by the Government's economic and financial policies?

More importantly – is the recovery balanced and sustainable? Have we achieved the fundamental economic reform needed to rid us of the spectre of a further disaster like the banking collapse? What are the key measures needed in the future to rebalance the economy? Is it enough to rely on extra revenues from the increase in GDP to help ordinary people, battered, unlike Chief Executives and financial whizz kids, by the economic situation?

These are vital questions for Liberal Democrats in particular who have invested so much political capital in the strategy of the Coalition government.

How it all happened

It is, of course, trite to say it all began with the Banks – and so it did. The banks created a gigantic bubble of unsustainable debt – fuelled primarily, not by government debt (despite the specific Greek problem), but by excessive private borrowing. There are, according to an article in the Economist,[6] "too many Zombie firms and over-indebted households".

"The euro zone's politicians, even in supposedly prudent Germany, have been reluctant to look too deeply into banks' balance-sheets, let alone to force them to clean themselves up. There are certainly questions to be asked about all the government bonds that the banks have bought in recent years. But the main dodgy assets that have been swept under the European carpet are private: bad loans made to households and companies."

The dodgy assets in turn were created by financial institutions which forgot both the ethics and the prudence on which the reputation and success of banks had been built for 300 years. The whole system was transformed into a sales model driven by ridiculous salaries and leveraged by a damaging bonus culture that was built on sand.

This process gathered pace, barely understood and perhaps quietly encouraged by governments dazzled by the dizzying tax revenues driven by financial engineering. In the United Kingdom, it was presided over by Tony Blair and

---

[6] Jon Berkley/SFP – The Economist 26th October 2013

Gordon Brown's New Labour government whose approach was light touch regulation. In a series of *mea culpa* speeches, the current shadow chancellor Ed Balls (who was a key economic figure in that Labour government) has accepted that Labour missed the key developments, not least the growing instability in the financial system, and failed to regulate the banks properly. But the apologies were more for political errors (that undoubtedly cost Labour electoral support) than for a decade and more of Blairite economic policy (that equally undoubtedly cost the country its prospects for the foreseeable future). There is still no recognition that the broader economic crisis had its roots not just in a simple regulatory failure but more in multiple failures that go to the core of the peculiar version of capitalism that New Labour remains wedded to.

But the Labour government's failure was not simply that of Pontius Pilate. Labour seemed and seems unable to wean itself off its dependence on the financial services sector. So Dr. Balls, do you want banks to stop rewarding failure, or continue to hand out paying exorbitant bonuses that feed into the near-collapse of the entire capitalist system as it represents much of your revenue stream? This contradiction was at the very heart of Labour's term in office – a dependence on impermanent revenue to shore up public spending, whether from one-off windfall taxes or volatile financial speculation. There's a depressing failure of imagination here.

Once the crisis happened, with the imminent ruin of RBS and Lloyds-TSB only hours away, most fair-minded commentators accept that the then Chancellor, Alistair Darling, acted with promptness and imagination to take over the banks and stabilise the situation – as did his counterparts in the US. The use of quantitative easing by the Bank of England is also generally thought to have been positive. It might not be hyper-critical, however, to say that Darling made one big mistake with which we are still living – namely the failure to restructure both executive pay and the banks themselves to better-serve the ailing economy. This was probably the one moment of time when this could have been done, given the panic that prevailed.

There are less flattering views. Sir Graham Watson, in his essay in this collection, gives much more credit to "swift action by the US Federal Reserve and the European Central Bank". Certainly the United States, with faster initial growth following the crash, more mortgage write-downs and a different attitude to bankruptcy, has managed to "unwind" more of the surplus and toxic debt than Europe.

What was the government strategy – and the alternatives?

The famous debates between the three party leaders at the 2010 general election showed differences of emphasis between Labour, the Conservatives and the Liberal Democrats but were characterised on all sides by an unwillingness to frighten the horses – a political caution in case an unguarded remark might spook the markets and blow the election. It is fair to say that Nick Clegg and Vince Cable had been ahead of most in warning of the potential problems of unsustainable levels of debt and in calling for a deficit reduction plan, but the full extent of the crisis did not enter the political debate until after the election.

The Liberal Democrats, as befits a party occupying the central political ground, navigated a middle way; our manifesto acknowledged the need to address the deficit in a way that didn't jeopardise the fragile recovery from the financial and economic meltdown we'd just suffered.

It's become a cliché to say this, but it bears repeating nonetheless – having failed to win the General Election, we weren't able to implement that plan in full; being in Coalition, we had to compromise around a plan both partners could agree to. So Plan A, as laid out in the Coalition Agreement, was a hybrid approach, reflecting Tory and Lib Dem priorities – committing to slower deficit reduction than the Tories would have pursued alone, in return for deeper cuts to welfare and student finance than the Lib Dems had previously countenanced.

It has also been clear throughout that, for all the political invective flung across the chamber of the House of Commons, all three parties made cutting the deficit in a reasonable timescale their self-determined test of credibility. The differences between Alistair Darling's strategy, George Osborne's strategy and the strategy offered by the Liberal Democrats at the election lay in the realm of small change in the overall approach.

The Conservative Party have always equated this crisis with the government's budget deficit. Their economic narrative, unchanged since well before the election, has been clear; public profligacy under Labour left us with an unmanageable deficit which, unless we eliminated it completely within this Parliament, would see bond traders pull their support and leave the UK as high and dry in the international markets as Greece or Portugal. Unable to offer a compelling counter-narrative, the coalition's junior partner settled for softening the edges of the damaging pace and nature of spending cuts that followed.

For almost 4 weary years after 2010, GDP crept along the bottom of the barrel, well below trend and lagging behind our more dynamic European neighbours; un(der)employment remained significant, with many of the jobs created being part-time and low-paid; inflation remained higher than planned; private-sector investment remained at an historic low; and throughout this an increasingly wealthy elite continued to take a bigger and bigger slice of the pie as pay, share options and profit. In other words, our economic problems went far, far deeper than the government's deficit; were we to eliminate the deficit overnight we'd still have an unbalanced, dysfunctional economy prone to further crashes.

Robert Skidelsky, in a very lucid article[7], demolished the theory of the "Swabian housewife" beloved of Angela Merkel – and of David Cameron and George Osborne. The Swabian housewife, asked about the collapse of Lehman Brothers in 2008, would, the German Chancellor said, "have told us that you cannot live beyond your means." This is the logic of austerity but it is fallacious because it ignore Keynes' "paradox of thrift": if everyone tries to save more in bad times, aggregate demand will fall, lowering total savings, because of the decrease in consumption and economic growth.

"If the government tries to cut its deficit," says Skidelsky, "households and firms will have to tighten their purse strings, resulting in less total spending. As a result, however much the government cuts its spending, its deficit will barely shrink. And if all countries pursue austerity simultaneously, lower demand for each country's goods will lead to lower domestic and foreign consumption, leaving all worse off." And so it proved.

Labour meanwhile has done what opposition parties are wont to do; far from acknowledging that they fell asleep at the wheel, they opposed every spending cut, sweeping under the carpet their own plans which committed them to nearly as many spending cuts as the Coalition. In calling for a Plan B, Labour appears curiously silent as to what that means. Essentially it boiled down to raising a small amount through higher taxes – which would leave the underlying economic structure intact, inviting yet more unequal and precarious growth.

---

[7] Four Fallacies of the Second Great Depression – Robert Skidelsky – Project Syndicate 20 November 2013

For much of the period since 2010, I and others called for a change of direction away from George Osborne's Plan A – not towards Labour's Plan B, which appeared less adequate the more we learnt about it (and we have stopped hearing anything about it now), but to a Liberal Democrat Plan C, a coherent vision of what a liberal democratic economy would look like and a roadmap as to how to get there. Plan C combined short-term boosts to investment by crowding in private-sector surpluses with a radical overhaul of our financial system and more long-term boosts to worker security and our skills base. Cutting the deficit using only direct approaches – reducing spending and raising taxes – wouldn't be as effective as a Kay-sian oblique approach[8] that puts dynamic and sustainable economic growth at its centre.

The core insight was that we needed to reform how our economy functions, following the failure of orthodox economic policy to deliver either prosperity for all during times of plenty or fairness in times of austerity. A nuanced diagnosis of what caused the ongoing financial crisis and the subsequent downturn in economic activity also has serious implications for how the government's budget deficit should be dealt with.

We began by proposing an approach to the fiscal deficit that was sensitive to a broad range of economic indicators, bringing government spending back in line with revenues in a manner compatible with sustainable rises in living standards. Our Plan C demanded priority for innovation, investment and infrastructure for jobs; fair finance fit for purpose; and building a flexible, adaptable economy which also provides security to individuals (which many in

---

[8] Professor John Kay is visiting Professor of Economics at the LSE and a Fellow of St. John's College, Oxford. He has postulated the "principle of obliquity" that economic goals are often best achieved indirectly.

continental Europe inelegantly described as a "flexicurity" economy).

Amongst other things we supported the separation of retail and investment banks in line with the Vickers Report on banking; the creation of **Public Interest Corporations** to deliver job-rich infrastructure projects and other solutions to economic challenges; the establishment of a **National Investment Bank**, with three distinct divisions to support housing, small to medium enterprises (SMEs) and export activity; establishing **publicly accountable regional banks**, and fostering a diverse and well-regulated ecosystem of alternative financial institutions such as credit unions, peer-to-peer lenders and local stock exchanges.

In order to develop our flexicurity economy, we called for increased workplace democracy to ensure that high pay is tackled through effective empowerment of workers and shareholders; a living wage; provision of robust employment insurance alongside appropriate skills training for those who fall out of work; help in substituting new employment for jobs lost to competitive pressures abroad; and a defined role for businesses, unions and employees in providing for an adaptable and secure workforce.

Of course none of us have ready-made answers, but we can argue for certain broad principles: that deficit reduction is merely a means to an end where our economy grows equitably and sustainably; that this end is jeopardised if we suck the economy dry of confidence, of Keynes' animal spirits; that public spending cuts won't automatically stimulate private investment without activist policy to foster it; and finally, that, unless we move towards a greener, more investment-based economic model, balanced government budgets and low interest rates alone won't prevent us sliding deeper into the mire.

The reality is that, while a chronic structural deficit is a burden on the public purse, there is no absolute optimum level of borrowing, of debt or of debt repayment – and therefore no magic elixir or eternal verity to be found in any particular level of government debt or deficit. Two further insights since the Social Liberal Forum first proposed an alternative economic strategy: the Bank of England's monetary stance has been hopelessly hamstrung by an unimaginative Treasury to raise nominal output, which is key to any recovery from a financial depression; and the corollary of a resilient labour market has been a shocking loss of productivity – which, if left unaddressed, will hamper prosperity for generations. Both deserve an essay in their own right!

What does the economy look like now?

The question of whether the strategies employed by successive governments in the wake of the 2008 crisis were successful, or could have been more successful with less pain, or whether different strategies would have risked an ongoing downward cycle of recession are now for the economic historian and it is still too early to make a definitive judgement. It is, however, well worth recounting the criticisms which many of us made at the time of those strategies.

The assessment made by the Social Liberal Forum was that the Coalition's central economic thesis – **that deficit reduction pursued mainly through spending cuts would lead to economy recovery** – was an inadequate response to the unresolved financial crisis of 2007/8 which left the economy stagnant, requiring a radical re-think of both fiscal and monetary policy.

It's worth reviewing what economic success looks like. To some, largely but not exclusively on the right of the political spectrum, the success of economic policy is judged by three metrics – inflation, GDP growth and budget deficits. To me, a successful economic strategy gives us more than these necessary but insufficient conditions. It gives us higher living standards, particularly for the less-well-off; less inequality; innovation backed by an Entrepreneurial State that helps us meet tomorrow's challenges; and a more sustainable way for us to make our living without compromising future generations' ability to meet their needs.

Recall that we aren't interested in output growth no matter how it's achieved – to repeat the mistakes of Labour and Tory governments of the past, and ignore the composition of said growth and the distribution of fruits from it, would be to invite a repetition of the crash of 2007/8 and subsequent depression.

Business Secretary Vince Cable, in an article on the same day as the comments quoted earlier from Nick Clegg[9], took a more nuanced approach. He warned that wages were not yet going up to match inflation, and described the Liberal Democrat approach:

"Deficit reduction alone was never going to be enough. That is why my Department has been working on a long-term plan to support companies growing and investing, job creation, and training our future workforce... At the heart of this has been a new industrial strategy for the UK which ... the Liberal Democrats (have) championed across government, building a stronger economy and a fairer society. ...We want to make sure that the UK is able to earn a living through our world-beating industries..... We aim to show that the UK is the right place to set up companies, invest and create long term jobs.

...But ...our recovery needs to be better balanced. Growth needs to be sustainable and we need every part of the UK to be firing on all cylinders... We cannot risk a repetition of the disastrous growth paths of the past when it depended on consumption financed by growing personal debt, depending in turn on inflated house prices. The emphasis must be on exports, investment and new technologies.

---

[9] Vince Cable – article on Liberal Democrat website 25,7,14

We must stop small and medium sized businesses being suffocated by the lack of bank credit..."

The UK economy has plainly suffered from a chronic lack of investment – unsurprising given the slashing of public capital spending over the coalition's first spending review, and the private sector's financial surplus of several hundred billion pounds. A report by the National Institute of Economic and Social Research (NIESR) showed that measures to reverse the dearth of investment would benefit the economy in both the short and medium term – the extent to which it would (and importantly the extent to which it wouldn't), suggested that a short-term, deficit-financed boost to investment is a necessary but insufficient condition for economic revival.

As Vince Cable recently set out, the balance of risks has shifted since Osborne's first budget, and government should fund large-scale investment by borrowing at the lowest rates on record. Further, it should take on the task of reforming the very roots of our political economy, moving beyond the sterile debate about borrowing into more radical territory that aids innovation, embeds fairness in the labour market and finally fixes the dysfunctional banking system.

It is true that the Coalition has, without saying as much, gradually mutated Plan A into something with at least a passing resemblance to our Plan C. The City Deals – including the most recent totalling over £1 billion investment to the Greater Glasgow conurbation – have softened the neglect of infrastructure publicly identified by Nick Clegg. Some progress has been made in dismantling the unwieldy size of the major banks. The landmark pension reforms, the much-vaunted rise in the tax threshold and the childcare plans in particular have helped with the cost of living issue for many families.

But several concerns arise. Much of the current 'recovery' remains based on consumer spending, which, as

Duncan Weldon points out, has increased despite an unprecedented drop in the value of earned income – as we dip into our savings to fund current spending. Absent a rise in household income – which has yet to materialise and to which we can add the alarming use of zero-hours contracts – reduced household savings cannot underpin a sustainable recovery. It can only lead us back to pre-crash levels of personal debt, and the financial cliff-edge we found ourselves on at that time.

Further, with government policy explicitly favouring a house price bubble, there is a real risk that rising service sector output, on the back of a wealth effect based on the same unstable pillars as before, masks the deepening crisis in living standards. Inequality might be lower today than in many previous years, but with most of the Coalition's benefits changes and the effect of underemployment since the crash yet to take hold, it is more than likely to rise in coming years – bringing with it the same damage to most people's capacity to live decent lives that preceded, perhaps even caused, the financial crash.

A central issue is the steady growth of inequality. The incomes of many people have stagnated whilst inflation erodes their living standards. Their power to earn a decent living from a hard day's work has steadily declined, which defies Buch's first law of political economy – that the primary purpose of a sustainable economy must be to empower all citizens to secure for themselves the means with which to live fulfilling lives they have reason to value.

There is little doubt that the richest have enjoyed far higher income growth than the poorest over the period both before and after the financial crisis – with the highest income decile a clear outlier and ordinary wages stagnant. No way are we all in it together!

The need for massive state spending in the form of tax credits and other benefits, to mask the failure of the labour market to provide a decent standard of living, also becomes clear – the Resolution Foundation Commission on Living Standards reckons the state effectively subsidises low wages to the tune of around £4bn a year, further distorting public finances in an effort to paper over serious fault lines in how the economy works.

The LSE's John van Reenen suggests that the low wage growth experienced by many isn't just masking the unemployment figures (which are held to be better than expected by most economic models) – lousy wages are holding back demand and impeding economic recovery – specifically lousy wage growth *amongst the lower half of the income distribution*.

What should the Banking Sector look like?

The banking crisis had, by 2011, cost the country £456.33 billion with Treasury exposure of £1.2 trillion – and £5 billion a year just to service the loan that the crisis incurred.[10] That is, of course, on top of crashing the real economy.

Despite an overall reduction in bonuses in the sector, a change of personnel at the top of many banks and the moves towards reducing their size, no one could claim with confidence that the problem of the banks has been solved and that never again can they threaten the future of our economy. In fact, average pay per head in 2012 was substantially higher than in 2007 just before the crash.[11] The Banking Commission itself said:

The discrepancy between the much-vaunted falls in bonuses and the reality of static or rising total and per-capita remuneration is in part due to a shift from variable to fixed pay.

Since the 'Big Bang' reforms to the UK's financial sector in the mid-1980s, mirrored by the piecemeal repeal of the

[10] Polly Curtis – The Guardian – 12th September 2011
[11] Parliamentary Commission on Banking Standards Report June 2013

Glass-Steagall reforms in the USA and a deregulatory race-to-the-bottom across the world, successive governments viewed ballooning profits in the financial services sector as an indication of the underlying health of the wider economy. As pillar after pillar of the financial house of cards crumbled, their failure showed these apparent profits to be based on a rotten core of under-priced risk and a crass failure to take account of systemic uncertainty.

However, those who wish to see integrated banks completely divest their retail arms should note that Lehmann Brothers had no retail activity and yet its failure caused seismic shockwaves that reverberate to this day. Also, several integrated banks survived without explicit taxpayer intervention (although all banks benefited from indirect State action such as the implied underwriting of retail deposits). Global financial crises are more likely to stem from the systemically risky behaviour of banks that are too big to fail. Or rather, too important to fail: the failure of even relatively small banks can be potentially disastrous, which is why the retail-only Northern Rock was saved from bankruptcy through nationalisation.

What does Good Banking look like?

The first thing a healthy economy requires from its financial services sector is sufficient and patient investment in capital-intensive areas of the economy where returns are uncertain but potentially transformative and/or able to strengthen public goods. This is part of the logic behind the Green Investment Bank championed by Liberal Democrats in the coalition. Job-intensive projects in the beefed-up Enterprise Zones should be prioritised for lending, as should measures to tackle energy efficiency, which pound-for-pound save more carbon emissions than the generation of power through renewable sources.

But we need too a broader-based National Investment Bank, organised to help three broad sectors of the economy (as is the case with the German KfW group of banks): housing, SMEs and the support of business-for-export. It would be able to take advantage of favourable borrowing conditions created by Treasury guarantees, and could be financed from increased tax receipts arising from a 'general anti-avoidance rule' that would bring in a fairer share of corporate profits; wealth taxes, such as those on high-value properties and on land values; and a 'financial transactions tax' (FTT). Although the globalised nature of finance makes such a tax difficult to implement in the absence of worldwide agreement, the 0.5% stamp duty that HMRC charges on shares traded in London shows that it would be possible at the domestic or EU-wide level, without leading to loss of business.

A network of publicly accountable regional banks should also be set up to provide credit and capital investment in innovation and for SMEs – investment that our current financial system is notoriously poor at providing - perhaps emerging from the break-up of the currently-nationalised RBS group. Such regional banks, arranged as mutuals or cooperatives, would have closer links to local businesses and a stake in their success, incentivising lending that leads to economic growth and job creation. The existence of a network of local and community banking institutions is crucial to economic revival. This will especially help if they act as the conduits for government schemes such as 'credit easing,' which currently fail to aid the wider economy because they rely on inadequate existing financial architecture, which remains out of touch with SMEs and still needs to repair its collective balance sheet before carrying out additional lending.

This network of new banks would form part of an ecosystem of financial institutions that encompasses credit unions, micro-finance providers, peer-to-peer lending facilities, local stock exchanges and other alternatives to traditional banking and investment. The Coalition has acted to encourage new entrants into the banking market, and the Business Bank has potential, but there's no transformative strategy at play.

The economy must become less dependent on debt and more on equity-finance. Policy in this area is likely to be very difficult and slow to implement, but working towards an equalisation of debt and equity in the tax system, as recommended in the Mirrlees review, would go a long way to ensuring that businesses are less dependent on ephemeral sources of credit and more on patient investment through equity-funding.

Towards a sustainable and fair future

Much of this essay has been on the theme of how to build a better and more sustainable economic and financial system following the 2008 financial collapse and its aftermath. We have spent some time on the macro-economics, on the banking structures and on the need for investment in infrastructure. Whilst I have been critical of the overall Government emphasis (whether under Labour or the Coalition) on obsessively pursuing a budget surplus by a target date – and the Conservative desire to carry this commitment forward into the next Parliament – it is clear that the Coalition has responded over time to some of the criticisms made by the Social Liberal Forum and others and that we now have a somewhat more balanced approach.

Business Secretary Vince Cable has, in several speeches, set out the Liberal Democrat approach: serious imbalances remain in the UK economy, so we need substantial investment in our creaking infrastructure and a recovery that sees sustainable prosperity reach beyond London and the South East. With house prices soaring in these regions – but stagnating elsewhere, along with job creation and productivity – it should come as no surprise that the recovery taking hold is of 'the wrong shape'. The only surprise is that pointing this out is seen as an act of coalition rebellion, not a warning to the country about the economic choices we face.

The essence of this approach is long term – enabling us to escape from an economic cycle based on financial markets and house prices. The Kay Review is looking at how financial institutions might change to "think long term". The Competition Commission should have more teeth. The banking landscape should change fundamentally. The European Commission should take action at a trans-national level against excesses of monopoly power by the global giants like Google, Microsoft and Amazon.

Since GDP began to grow again, many on the right have claimed vindication for current policy. Even Vince Cable now suggests (I'm paraphrasing) that the Keynesian moment has passed and that we're now into "how to share the spoils" territory. I would argue that most of the 'recovery' to date has been cyclical and unstable; that the underlying issues of power and accountability in the economy remain unsolved, and that fiscal and monetary policy remains unaligned with achieving green, sustainable and innovative growth.

Nevertheless, it is a welcome change if government feels it has more room for manoeuvre to build on the tax and pension reforms that Liberal Democrats have brought to the Coalition to help ordinary people who feel battered by the cost of living challenges of the last 6 years. A key element though of a credible economic platform is to support investment and the growth of incomes. So I want the Chancellor to use the power he has under the Bank of England Act 1998 to ask the Bank to tackle weak income growth – ensuring that the bank takes the principle of QE and puts real muscle behind measures to invest in long-term growth.

There is a strengthened role too for the High Pay Commission to prevent executive top pay leap frogging. Institutional shareholders should be made more accountable

– many are simply exercising without accountability the enormous power that comes with running *our* pension or endowment funds - and the reserve power to force them to disclose how they voted should be brought into effect.

It is at this point that a central principle of social liberalism comes into play – that a liberal, accountable and open state should act as a countervailing force to the inequality that results when the market's' invisible hand' distorts outcomes through unjust practices – better put in the words of L.T. Hobhouse in 1911:

The function of the State is to secure conditions upon which its citizens are able to win, by their own effort, all that is necessary to a full civic efficiency. It is for the State to take care that the economic conditions are such that the normal man who is not defective in mind or body or will can by useful labour feed, house and clothe himself and his family.[12]

---

[12] L. T. Hobshouse, in Liberalism (1911)

The Folly of High Pay

Duncan Exley

The concept of a 'fair day's pay for a fair day's work' is familiar to most people. The idea that if you work hard and put in the effort then that effort should be rewarded – this is seen by almost everyone as fair and just. But for many the reality of working life is something very different. Long working hours, rising costs and stagnating real wages have become the norm for a worrying, and increasing, number of workers. At the same time, a tiny 'elite' is hoovering up gargantuan wages and vast wealth.

To illustrate the point, those who manage our biggest companies are typically paid over £4 million a year; it would take someone on a Living Wage around 375 years to earn just a year's worth of this pay. Unsurprisingly there is little concrete evidence to prove these pay differentials are a result of value, intelligence or hard work. In fact, if anything, both the super-rich and the increasingly impoverished 'rest' have seen their wages decoupled from their actual economic value. The result is that the UK is now one of the developed world's most unequal countries in terms of income and wealth.

An economic chasm has appeared between people at the top and the rest, and the impact on our economy is increasingly obvious. One in five workers in the UK is now low-paid, one of the worst rates among OECD countries. Many of the jobs people find themselves in effectively trap them in poverty; in fact the majority of people in poverty are now in working households. Increases in consumer spending, traditionally a reliable driver of economic growth, are not likely to be sustainable and the pressures on household budgets are seeing more people in financial difficulty. There will be a major problem, as various commentators have observed, if current low interest rates, themselves arguably at too low levels, were to rise. This is no way to build a stable, sustainable, and strong economy.

But the implications go much further. Studies have shown how more unequal countries have worse life expectancy, health, educational outcomes, social mobility and crime. In 2014, the UK faces a culture of huge inequality in pay, wealth and power that threatens to destabilise not only our economy, but our wider society as well. Organisations including the IFS predict this inequality will continue to rise sharply in the coming years.

The Politics of Pay Inequality

This is also a political issue. The success of UKIP has shown that parties can make headway by positioning themselves as "the people's army" in opposition to real or imagined "elites". Similarly there is a flipside, with a genuine risk to any party who can be painted as being too cosy with these self-serving elites. Increasingly it seems the business community is viewed as one such group. Recent polling by the FT found that a majority want action taken against big businesses. The financial crash may have caused opprobrium at the activities of financial services organisations, but it seems it may also have helped to foment a more worrying general mistrust of business.

Politicians are walking a dangerously thin tight-rope when they allow themselves to be perceived as colluding with those who champion the concept of 'wealth creators' and 'top talent', while writing off the rest of us.

Rise of the 'super-manager'

In order to identify the best solutions to reduce inequality, it is important to understand its root causes. One of the undoubted reasons behind rising pay inequality is the huge increase in executive pay at the top, and the rise of the so-called 'super-manager'.

In the last 40 years, the richest 1% have seen their share of income increase substantially. One of the driving forces behind this is the emergence of the 'super-manager', a small group of executives receiving an increasing share of income and constituting a large and increasing proportion of the top 1%.

A number of reasons have been given for this. Perhaps the most frequent claim in political and economic debate is that such high-income super-managers justify their pay as they provide exceptionally high marginal productivity. In other words, they're worth it. However, the academic evidence doesn't back this up.

Super-managers and marginal productivity

"We looked at tens of thousands of interviews, and everyone who had done the interviews and what they scored the candidate, and how that person ultimately performed in their job. We found zero relationship. It's a complete random mess, except for one guy who was highly predictive because he only interviewed people for a very specialized area, where he happened to be the world's leading expert."

The above quote from Google's Senior Vice President of People Operations[13] illustrates a key problem in selecting the right candidate for a role. Even some of the best recruiters cannot say that they are secure in the knowledge that the chosen candidate is the best person to do the job, unless

---

[13] New York Times 19th June 2013

there is a very specific skill-set needed to deal with a very specific problem.

Executive recruitment is not exempt from this problem. Senior managers require a wide variety of skills for a large collection of non-specific tasks. As a consequence, such roles are very difficult to recruit for. The methods used to recruit CEOs and senior management provide little reason to think that the most talented person is selected for the job.[14] While this problem may not in itself be unique to CEOs and senior management, recruitment of senior management is associated with an additional problem, specific to the industry: it is difficult to determine an executive's effectiveness even following their recruitment.

A key measure to assess an employee's productivity is the degree to which their role is replicable. Situations in which there are many people performing the same job make it relatively simple to identify whether one person is performing the job better than another. The jobs of super-managers, however, are not replicable as they differ vastly both between different companies and over time. To make matters worse, it is obvious that this could not be solved by experimenting with many different people doing the same job in a short period of time.[15]

It is difficult to square the above finding with the assertion that companies are rewarding an individual's performance with increased pay packages. If performance can't be measured, how can pay reflect performance? This assertion is further undermined by a study of variance between different CEO's pay in cases where there had been a change of CEO. The authors found that firm culture and other firm specific effects accounted for just under $2m of variance within annual compensation, while individual

---

[14] Jacquart, Armstrong 2013
[15] Piketty 2014

manager effects accounted for \$2.5m of compensation variance.[16] Crucially, this does not imply that the talent of individual managers accounts for this \$2.5m variation but rather that the variation is attributable to any individual factors that differentiate them from other CEOs; this could simply be their ability to bargain for higher pay.

The evidence, therefore, suggests that talent doesn't necessarily determine pay and that other factors play a large role. Some evidence even suggests that increasing pay actually decreases productivity.[17]

Executive Pay and Technology

The assertion that senior managers do not add sufficient value to justify their pay is controversial and disputed by a number of prominent economists. Greg Mankiw presents the most well-known defence of the value added by the top 1%. He asserts that the top 1% receive their high incomes because they add an amount of value that is equivalent to, or higher than, their high salary.

Mankiw suggests that the dramatic increase in top incomes is mainly attributable to technology; this has allowed for an increase in efficiency and, crucially, only a small number of people have the skills and education to take advantage of this new opportunity. Mankiw argues that models which assume that a good CEO is simply hugely valuable for a company provide the best account of why CEO pay has risen.[18] Other economists have added to this account by suggesting that innovators and highly paid managers increase the productivity of the whole workforce.[19]

But there are problems with Mankiw's account of the reasons for excessively high pay at the top. Some increases in

---

[16] Graham, Li and Qiu 2012
[17] Jacquart, Armstrong 2013
[18] Mankiw 2013
[19] Ozimek 2011

inequality may be explained by technology providing additional gains to highly educated people. However this does not explain the increasing gap between the top 10% and the top 1% where, research suggests, there is little difference in education.[20]

Mankiw's argument rests on the assumptions that the labour market is working perfectly and that wages are allocated correctly by the market. However, there does not appear to be evidence that this is true. Given that there is 'informational dissymmetry' (wage setters don't know the productivity of their employees), there seems to be good reason to doubt that the market is working efficiently.

Executive Pay and Company Value

Others have looked to see if there is a link between executive pay and company size. There are two competing explanations of the link between firm size and executive compensation. One states that larger organisations require more talented executives in order to manage them and so are compensated more highly. The other explanation suggests that this is simply a market failure and there has been no downward pressure on executive wages to counteract the rigidity effects of compensation. It is far from clear that the value of a CEO increases at the same rate as a company increases in size. A company that doubles in size doesn't necessarily get twice as much value from their CEO. Nor is it clear that the market for those who could serve as an executive for that much larger a company decreases in the same proportion.

Executive Pay and Bargaining Power

The argument that increasing executive pay is largely attributable to managerial power and bargaining has become popular in recent years. But there are several problems with this explanation. In particular, these theories suggest that

---

[20] Piketty 2014

executives have essentially gained control of pay setting bodies and are in effect partly setting their own pay, implying that more independent pay setting bodies would reduce pay for executives.

However research suggests that there is no relationship between board or compensation committee structure and executive pay. The theories on managerial power and bargaining would suggest that consultants working for management would be more likely to increase pay, however research has found that it was consultants working for the Board who were more likely to do so.[21]

An alternate and more persuasive explanation is one based on the "Lake Wobegon" effect.[22] Companies want the best talent and are recommended by their compensation consultant to set their remuneration packages to be above the average, often in the upper quartile. Overall, this has the effect of increasing the average compensation as each company seeks to be above average.[23] This idea of a common culture in remuneration is supported by the finding that in the US only five consultancy firms control 50% of the market on compensation consultancy.[24]

A Low-Pay, Low-Skill Economy

While executives may be able to demand higher and higher incomes, the rest have not been so lucky. Real wages for many have stagnated and for some have even fallen. Buoyant employment figures have largely distracted us from the problem of low wages, but the reality is that the UK workforce is low-paid, low-skilled and has low productivity. We have a higher proportion of low-skilled jobs than any

---

[21] Conyon 2014
[22] http://en.wikipedia.org/wiki/Lake_Wobegon#The_Lake_Wobegon_effect
[23] Dew-Backer, Gordon 2005
[24] Conyon 2014

other OECD country except Spain,[25] the fifth highest proportion of workers in low-paid jobs out of 25 OECD countries,[26] and the second lowest productivity of the G7 countries.[27]

The UK economy is also worryingly unbalanced towards London and the South East and towards the service sector, which creates damaging regional inequalities in prosperity, housing, employment and types of jobs. The median income in London is 28% higher than the national average and 41% higher than in Wales.[28] The average house price in London as of February 2014 was £428,000, up 17.7% in 12 months. This compared to £181,000 in Scotland, up only 2.3% over the same period.[29] London has outperformed the rest of the UK for job creation since 2008. The number of jobs in London since March 2008 has increased 8.9% compared to just 0.5% in the UK as a whole.[30]

The low-skill and low-pay jobs that have blossomed since the financial crash aren't simply entry-level jobs, a first rung on the employment ladder that can be climbed through industry and intelligence. Most are career cul-de-sacs with little chance of progression or promotion. The language around pay perhaps highlights the problem. While executive pay is described as 'talent retention' or an investment, pay for everyone else is described as a 'cost to be reduced'.

---

[25] Skills Outlook 2013, OECD, 2013
[26] Resolution Foundation, 2013, Low Pay Britain 2013, p14-5
[27] ONS, 2014, International Comparisons of Productivity
http://www.ons.gov.uk/ons/rel/icp/international-comparisons-of-productivity/2012---
final-estimates/info-icpfeb14.html
[28] ONS, 2013, Annual Survey of Hours and Earnings, 2013 Provisional results
[29] ONS House Price Index, February 2014
[30] ONS, Labour Market Statistics May 2014

Our systems of management and industrial relations are also unfit for purpose in the 21st century. We place far too little emphasis on training and developing managers compared to other European countries: 70% of managers report that their firms don't offer them a career development structure.[31] Lack of regard for people-management suggests a mind-set that fails to recognise that a business relies upon the efforts of its entire staff. In recent decades senior executives have absorbed an increasing share of the payroll, but rarely seek to promote workforce 'ownership' of company strategy. The result is a collapse in trust between employer and employee. Over half of employees (56%) agree that "management will always try to get the better of employees if it gets the chance" and only 17% disagree.[32] A third of employees say that their level of trust in senior management is weak.[33]

Poverty Pay

There are now 279,000 people paid below the National Minimum Wage[34]. Extensive research has shown the long-term physical and mental health effects of low pay[35], which in turn create huge costs for the taxpayer. Most people in poverty are in working households, and it is estimated that child poverty costs the taxpayer £29 billion per year

---

[31] Mabey, Chris and Ramirez, Matias (2012) 'Comparing national approaches to management development. In: Handbook of Research on Comparative Human Resource Management'. Edward Elgar, pp. 185-210. ISBN 978-1847207265

[32] Natcen, 2013, British Social Attitudes 30, http://bsa-30.natcen.ac.uk/media/24859/bsa_30_annotated_questionnaire_2012.pdf

[33] CIPD, Oct 2013 Employee Outlook: Focus on trust in leaders,

[34] ONS, April 2013 Low Pay Estimates http://www.ons.gov.uk/ons/rel/ashe/low-pay/april-2013/stb-2013-low-pay-estimates.html

[35] Zacchaeus 2000, 2011, 'The Descent into Negative Welfare'

including £1.26 billion spent on the justice system and £2.75 billion spent on children's social services.[36]

This poverty pay doesn't just affect those receiving it. Both the IMF and OECD now recognise the dangers to economic growth of huge inequality in incomes and wealth between ordinary employees and those at the top. Some of the reasons why our excessively high levels of pay inequality are holding back growth are simple common sense. A high prevalence of low pay and insecure pay suppresses consumer driven growth and/or fuels debt. UK consumers have too low a disposable income to drive recovery without amassing unsustainable debt. Almost a third of UK families have savings of less than £500.[37] Due to the widely differing incidences of low pay between UK regions, low pay and consequent low consumer spending further exacerbates regional inequality. Average weekly household spend in London is 40% higher than in the North East for example.

In addition, the prevalence of low-cost labour has effectively incentivised businesses not to invest in technology and skills. A vicious cycle has been created, where taxpayers subsidise artificially low pay, low-skill jobs through the social security system, making it less attractive for businesses to invest in the alternative approach of staff development training or innovation.

Contrary to many assertions, a low National Minimum Wage may also *suppress* employment rates. As one assessment of the issue suggests: "once the potential macroeconomic stimulus effects of extending the living wage to all employees

---

[36] 0 Hirsch, 2013, 'An estimate of the cost of child poverty in 2013' http://www.cpag.org.uk/sites/default/files/Cost%20of%20child%20poverty%20research%20update%20(2013).pdf

[37] Aviva, 2013, 'Growing family incomes disguise widening gap and slender savings buffer', http://www.aviva.co.uk/media-centre/story/17249/growing-family-incomes-disguise-widening-gap-and-s/

are taken into account, it is more likely than not that a statutory living wage would result in a modest boost to aggregate employment".[38]

Income Inequality and Tax

Pay inequality, and high pay at the top, is not helped by the UK tax system. Our relatively progressive income tax masks a darker truth – that when all taxes on income are taken into account, the UK tax system is in fact hopelessly regressive.

Research conducted by The Equality Trust found that the poorest 10% pay 43% of their income in tax compared to 35% for the richest 10%[39] – the poorest being hit harder proportionally by taxes such as VAT and council tax. This has not been helped by the return of a 45p top rate of income tax, which has effectively given a big bonus to the richest 1%.

Polling conducted in partnership with Ipsos MORI found a worrying lack of public awareness of what people on different incomes are taxed. On average, people vastly underestimate what the poorest 10% pay in tax, believing it to be just 24%. They believe they should pay just 15%. A staggering 96% support a more progressive tax system than our current one.

In essence, our tax system is confusing, unfair and unpopular, and is a driver of income inequality.

What are the Solutions?

Pay and income inequality is a complex problem. There is no silver bullet policy that can immediately bring about its reduction. However, there are policies that could start us towards a more equal, prosperous, healthier and happier society. The fact that no policy has come close in the last 30

---

[38] Reed, 2013, 'The Economic Impact of Extending the Living Wage to all Employees in the UK'

[39] http://www.equalitytrust.org.uk/sites/default/files/attachments/resources/Unfair%20and%20Unclear_0.pdf

years to bringing UK inequality towards the OECD average should be a cause of extreme concern and embarrassment to our politicians and policymakers.

One of the biggest challenges the UK faces is that, at almost all points, the poorest in society have barriers erected to their move up the ladder. They are systemically and systematically prevented from narrowing the economic gap between themselves and those above them. A number of these barriers have been erected, deliberately or otherwise, by the very richest in society.

Fair Taxes

Taxation is no longer a vogue mechanism with which to reduce inequality. It is true that simple taxation policies alone are unlikely to reduce inequality, but it is untrue that they have no part to play.

The Equality Trust's own research[40] has shown that increasing the top rate of tax could decrease the share of income going to the top 1% without damaging economic growth, and may in fact strengthen the economy.[41] Moreover, 55% of the electorate think that rich people are not paying enough tax and should pay more.[42] A majority support a top rate of income tax of 50p or more. A return to a 50p top rate of income tax is popular and economically sound and must be considered by politicians.

Unearned income, and the rise in property and wealth inequality is also an important area that must be challenged. Council tax should be transformed into a progressive property tax by re-evaluating properties and creating new bands with higher rates for high value properties. A

---

[40] http://www.equalitytrust.org.uk/resources/our-publications/course-correction-pre-distributive-case-50p-top-income-tax-rate

[41] Equality Trust 2014, 'Course correction: The pre-distributive case for the 50p top tax rate'

[42] Yougov/Sunday Times poll, 30 September 2012

progressive property value tax would reduce the size of median gross bills by £279 a year compared to the Council Tax we have now.[43]

Fair Pay

Perhaps the simplest way to tackle pay and income inequality is to go straight to the source. Some of the UK's worst-paid jobs are among the most vital to our society, including nursery nurses and care workers. They should be sufficiently paid and respected so that people actively choose them as a career path.

No employer should be able to pay a wage that prevents an employee from acquiring adequate food, fuel and accommodation. All jobs should pay enough for people to live in dignified circumstances. The main UK parties have voiced aspirations to raise the National Minimum Wage (NMW) to £7.00 or link its value to median pay[44]; this is a step forward, but should not be regarded as an end point

There is evidence that extending the Living Wage to all employees would bring benefits to taxpayers, employees and employers. The rate of National Minimum Wage (NMW) should therefore be increased to a Living Wage, with costs shared between employers, government and those with excessively high incomes. Government would bear some of this cost by raising the lower limit of employer and employee National Insurance contributions as the minimum wage rises. Part of this cost to Government would be offset by raising the upper limit of National Insurance contributions.

[43] Chris Leishman et al., 2014, 'After the Council Tax: Impacts of Property Tax Reform on People Places and House Prices', JRF
http://www.jrf.org.uk/publications/council-tax-impacts
[44] BBC, 2014, 'Osborne wants above-inflation minimum wage rise'
http://www.bbc.co.uk/news/uk-politics-25766558 and Buckle, 2014, 'Low Pay: The nation's challenge'
http://www.yourbritain.org.uk/uploads/editor/files/Alan_Buckle_revie
w_FINAL_20May20142.pdf

In addition, the Low Pay Commission should be given forward guidance that the NMW should increase to the level of the equivalent Living Wage.

Additionally, we remain unconvinced that HMRC *alone* can enforce the NMW. Indeed they have to date made a pretty poor job of it, with only 9 employers ever prosecuted for paying below NMW (despite evidence that almost 300,000 people in the UK are paid below this rate). Local authorities should be given powers and resources to prosecute National Minimum Wage evasion, and given a proportion of the fines. Local Authorities should also be given powers to charge daily default fines for employers that are found to be avoiding the National Minimum Wage. Such measures would take advantage of local authorities' local knowledge, while giving them the incentive and means to carry out this work, and this would also allow greater accountability of enforcement to civil society.

Fairer Pay and a Stronger Society

There is a temptation to see inequality as inevitable, a natural consequence of people's unequal abilities. But the reality is that over the past 30 years, inequality has been exacerbated by political and economic policy decisions.

Inequality today is at damagingly high levels, harming people's health and wellbeing, and stifling our economic recovery. It is driving the growth in personal debt, and fuelling an economy based on debt and volatility.

A rising tide does not necessarily lift all boats. In today's UK wealth is not trickling down. Politicians and businesses can no longer avoid the consequences of inequality on an increasingly angry and frustrated electorate.

But political action can reverse this inequality. By creating a system that increases opportunities for all, with fair pay, fairer businesses and fair tax, we can build a society that is happier, healthier and stronger. We can also build an economy that provides stable, long-term growth that benefits all.

We therefore call on all political parties to commit to one simple aim; to include in their manifestos an explicit goal that the net impact of their policies will be to reduce the gap between the richest and the rest.

Towards a Liberal welfare system

Robert Aldridge

The radical welfare reforms underway at present have led to an outpouring of outrage – some justified but some simply a reaction to change. However cack-handed some of the reforms may have been, they have at least raised fundamental questions about the role of welfare benefits in the 21st century, although at the same time they have uncovered and reinforced some awful and largely unfounded prejudices about those who make claims upon the system.

The reforms ostensibly were about a welfare budget which was growing and considered to be 'out of control.' The implication was that the system was awash with fraudulent claims and people who were workshy. Whilst any system contains people who misuse it and every effort must be made to prevent that, the demonisation of those reliant on benefit undermines the vast majority of claimants who simply are in need of support because of circumstances beyond their control. An initial step in a Liberal welfare approach should be to re-establish respect and dignity for those who have to rely on the welfare system for whatever reason.

There is a massive irony in the fact that the biggest growth in welfare payments in recent years has been in 'in work' benefits, tackling relative poverty rather than absolute poverty. In effect a significant proportion of the welfare budget simply subsidises (from the public purse) employers who either cannot or will not pay staff enough to live on. It may be that, if our industries are to be competitive or if we want to maintain employment levels, the state will have to continue to subsidise employers either directly or, as is currently the case, indirectly through subsidising the employees who do not earn enough to live on. However, this is neither in the spirit of free competition within the EU, nor is it the role most people expect of the welfare system. It certainly has nothing to do with the caricature of the 'something for nothing' claimant lying in bed all day. If the task is to reduce or limit the welfare budget the most logical way to do so is to ensure it has a clear remit and does not suffer from the 'mission creep' which has led to such a large proportion of payments being made, for example, to people in work. If the problem lies in a need to subsidise employment, policies should be developed to manage that rather than confusing it with welfare.

Part of the solution may lie in promotion of the 'Living Wage' and continuing to use the tax system to benefit those on low pay. Part may lie in ensuring that significant cost of living issues such as childcare, energy and housing costs are controlled and appropriate means found to ensure that the essentials for living are affordable. But part of it is about a steady move to a less unequal society where pay differentials are not so great to enable those paid least to live off their income rather than having to rely on a combination of their income and state assistance. The aim must be to make work pay rather than to make work pay some and the state pay the rest.

However, this is far from easy to achieve. One of the clear obstacles when people leave the benefit system is the rate at which benefit is withdrawn. The nett benefit to the individual for every £1 earned is only a few pence. Recent reforms to thresholds at which individuals start to pay income tax have been welcome for those at the slightly higher end of low earnings, but have made no difference to those on very low incomes who were not paying tax before the reforms. A focus on helping to make work pay more than it does at present for those on very low incomes will need to focus on the taper. The Universal Credit system attempts to simplify the inter-relationship between benefits which should be helpful, but ultimately the steep rate at which benefits are removed should be made less severe.

This of course links to the question of subsidising employers and is a complex area not only in terms of principle but also operationally to avoid perverse anomalies arising. It also requires careful management to avoid a situation where someone in transition from the welfare benefit system is better off than someone who has entered employment directly without previously being reliant on benefits.

One of the more distasteful elements of the new welfare system is the fundamental shift from a system based on entitlements according to need, to one which is based on the claimant having to earn their benefit. The new 'claimant commitment' is a kind of contract which a claimant signs with the DWP to undertake certain activities in order to obtain their benefit. They only receive their benefit if they comply with that contract. The term 'conditionality' is used by government, and benefit sanctions are imposed if a claimant does not fulfil the contract. This often includes making work search a full time occupation for 30 hours per week, or volunteering which has to be undertaken, for example.

The concept appears to have a parallel with that of the Victorian workhouse where assistance was conditional on working. It is sad that we have returned to a subjective and judgmental system based on 'deserving' and 'undeserving' poor and one in which claimants become supplicants whose entitlement to benefit is dependent upon whether the department believes he or she has done enough to deserve their benefit.

Not only is it a more subjective system than the one it replaced, with a great deal of discretion and power in the hands of individual benefits assessors, but it clearly disempowers individuals dependent upon the welfare system. A Liberal welfare system should be non judgmental, based upon entitlements and conditional on need, rather than whether an individual 'deserves' or has 'earned' the right to help.

There is clearly a tension between seeking to have a system which can be tailored to an individual's needs and which therefore must incorporate an element of subjectivity and discretion, with one in which the claimant has rights and can have a clear and objective basis for appeal if it appears a decision is unfair. The reforms place a great deal of power with individual workers and make it difficult to establish objective grounds if a claimant wishes to appeal. The balance must be adjusted. It is perfectly possible to have a clear framework of rights and entitlements with an element of discretion enabling individual tailoring as an add-on.

The evidence that the current balance is wrong can be evidenced from the exponential growth in the number of benefits 'sanctions' imposed. A sanction – i.e. the removal of welfare benefits – can last 3 weeks, 3 months or 3 years. If a welfare system is to have sanctions as part of it, and it is questionable whether they have any real beneficial value, a sanction should only be imposed for the most serious cases. This is clearly not the case in the current regime, where sanctions appear to be intended more as a means of persuading affluent Middle England that the government is not a 'soft touch' rather than making a meaningful contribution to helping people back into work. Indeed sanctions appear to be throwing many people into further sustained poverty due to the time it takes to recover financially from the loss of income.

That is not to say that all of the elements in the reforms are bad. It is extremely positive that people's capacity for work is considered and that they are not written off as 'incapable.' It is also positive that there is greater support for people entering the workforce after a long period of absence. Helping people to maximise their potential is a fundamental of Liberalism. However, handing out a financial punishment if they fail to do so is not, and should not form part of any welfare system.

There has been considerable discussion about what has been termed the Scandinavian model of welfare, which is based around relatively generous universal benefits. The system in the UK is a hybrid, with some elements which are universal (e.g. child benefit [to all intents and purposes], state pension) but most of which are targeted at specific areas of need. Targeting welfare at those who need it, provided that it can be done effectively, appears the most efficient and affordable approach. However, it relies on other elements outside the welfare system in order to be effective, such as employers paying a living wage and affordable general living costs, especially childcare and household energy costs.

The reforms have also deliberately missed a massive and significant sector of benefit recipients – pensioners. It is perhaps understandable that for pragmatic reasons and short term political expediency successive governments have avoided changes which impact on this group. After all they are the ones who are most likely to vote. However at least for the short term they comprise a group who are relatively comfortable, if they have a pension beyond the state pension.

If we really are 'all in this together' then those who are already over pensionable age and who are financially comfortable must be part of that. There are significant numbers of relatively wealthy pensioners – the pre baby boom generation – a considerable number of whom are in receipt of index linked final salary scheme or other relatively generous pensions. This may not be the case in the medium or long term, but provides a short term window to enable longer term policies to be developed in which welfare assistance is targeted at those who require it.

Whilst there are clear health and social advantages to those reliant on the basic pension to get a range of additional benefits, it is hard to justify that those who are financially comfortable receive the various 'universal' benefits, including free bus travel, winter heating allowances etc. Indeed some high profile wealthy pensioner celebrities have already expressed outrage that, whilst some people are using food banks, they are unable even to opt out of their universal benefits.

It is another irony that the 'bedroom tax' which was introduced to encourage people to downsize to more appropriately sized accommodation did not apply to pensioners who represent a significant proportion of those under-occupying properties and for whom the government is still prepared to pay what it terms its 'spare room subsidy.' It is perverse to exclude them from the policy (though the policy itself is fundamentally flawed). There are parts of the country, though generally not in Scotland, where families have to wait considerable periods for rented accommodation of the right size. In those cases those under-occupying such properties should be encouraged to move to more appropriately sized properties. However, there is no logical reason why the pool of people should be restricted to those of working age.

Housing costs have been one area which has been the focus of attention with a range of relatively *ad hoc* reforms. Whilst there is a superficial simplicity and logic in moving towards applying the same rules for rent subsidy to the social and private rental sectors, it is impractical for a number of reasons. Not least is the role we expect the social rented sector to play in housing those in the greatest housing need. Social housing has traditionally been financed through capital and revenue subsidies – the former through grant funding towards the building of houses and the latter through rent subsidies (housing benefit). Rents in social housing are generally below market and pose no threat to the rent subsidy budget. Generally it is more important that people are able to live in secure and stable accommodation of a decent standard to start rebuilding their lives, rather than whether they have an extra bedroom.

Rents in the private rented sector depend on the market and vary dramatically from area to area. Arbitrary rules have been introduced largely to tackle problems which have arisen in the private rental market in London, but which are far less of a problem elsewhere in the UK.

It is not logical that the national system has been skewed to manage a problem in London rather than tackling that problem as a regional London issue or one which only affects a limited number of regional hotspots. Given that the number of regional 'hot spots' is very limited a balance must be found to ensure that regional differences are recognised, that those reliant on benefits can still access the private rented sector and that landlords can still achieve a rate of return on their business.

It would be worth considering as part of this the imposition of rent regulation. This could be introduced governing either or both of two aspects of private renting. At one level it could ensure that any annual rent increases in the private rented sector are restricted. That would bring greater stability to the part of the rent subsidy budget which is causing concern, without denying access to private renting to people on benefits. Another level would be to consider setting levels or bands within which initial rents would have to be set (linked to quality, size etc). The latter could have quite a significant impact, but could also lead to unintended consequences, such as a reduction in the number of landlords willing to let. So this would require careful testing prior to any roll out nationally.

Underlying all reforms has been a concern that the welfare budget is running out of control. It has not been established that this is in fact the case. Of course, during a period of recession reliance on benefit will increase, but demand will also decrease as the economy expands, provided that employers are paying wages which enable employees to cover their living costs. Linked to the questionable contention that the budget has been out of control, has been a continuing move to 'cap' or cash limit various parts of the welfare budget.

This approach runs counter to how a Liberal welfare regime should function. The principle should be that those in need and who fit the criteria should be entitled to assistance i.e. a system which is demand led rather than cash limited. If demand begins to run out of control, it suggests a failure in policies which are contributing to that need. The solution should generally be to tackle the cause of the policy failure rather than limiting help to those who are suffering as a result.

The attitude to welfare by successive governments has become confused and corrupted. The focus has been on the small minority who abuse the system rather than the vast majority who need and use the welfare system to live a civilised life. The temptation has been to demonise and caricature claimants as workshy scroungers in order to justify elements of welfare policy which are illogical, unfair and which subjugate claimants into supplicants dependent on the goodwill and subjective decisions of individual staff members. As a result the positive elements – of supporting people into work, focusing on their capacity rather than their incapacity, and simplifying a hugely complex system – have been undermined.

The analyses of the problems which face the welfare system have been internalised – restricted only to looking at the welfare system itself. A Liberal solution needs not only to build on the positive elements of the existing reforms and re-examine the fundamental principles to ensure the basics are fair, just and respectful of people in need, but also to look beyond the welfare system for some of the solutions, which lie in a combination of other policy areas including high living costs and low incomes.

The UK, Europe
and the World

Scotland and Britain
after the Referendum

David Steel

It is an interesting speculation whether the referendum on Scottish independence will prove to be the defining moment for this generation as the First World War and the Second World War were for my generation and those of my father and grandfather.

The curious timing of this book of essays mean that I write these words before the outcome of the referendum is known but with publication taking place after the result – a recipe for confounded predictions, if ever there was one! Will it have been a vindication of the power of nationalism even in the 21st century, or, as I hope, a reaffirmation of a successful and productive multi-national union?

Referenda

I am not a great believer in referenda. Despite being ostensibly about one major issue, they tend to get mixed up – as has occurred with this referendum too – with people's views about the Government of the day, the state of the economy or other general discontents. Nevertheless the referendum has become established in UK political practice as being suited to the determination of major constitutional issues, and the nearest thing we have in this country so far to constitutional entrenchment.

But it is already clear that the Scottish referendum which has obsessed, bored, stimulated and excited the population for many, many months has also been a unique event which has changed and will change the terms of constitutional and political debate both in Scotland and across the whole of Britain for many years to come.

The Edinburgh Agreement

It is worthy of note that the arrangements for the referenda were agreed between the UK Government and the Scottish Government – in stark contrast to the stand off on this issue between the Spanish and Catalan governments, far less the unilateral referendum held on the future of the Crimea.

The "Edinburgh Agreement" was negotiated and secured by Michael Moore as Secretary of State for Scotland – and, if some of the work of the Coalition remains highly controversial, Michael's achievement is a testament both to his own sterling qualities and to the value of having an able Liberal Democrat in post at a crucial time. It was a model of its kind.

I am not sure if Michael was aware of the judgement of the Supreme Court of Canada following the Quebec separatist referendum – they concluded that the National Assembly, legislature or government of Quebec do not have, either under Canadian law or international law, the right to effect the secession of Quebec from Canada unilaterally. However, the rest of Canada would have a political obligation to negotiate Quebec's separation if a clear majority of that province's population voted in favour of it.

That seems to me an excellent legal view on how secession by one part of a country affects the rest of the country, but how ultimately the right of self determination should prevail.

Quislings and Liars

It has been distressing to see the extent to which so many protagonists on either side have been prepared to characterise their opponents as liars, cheats, Quislings, dishonest, self seeking or deluded – or alternatively to rant and shout their opponents down. Some of this is commonplace in politics but some of the referendum exchanges took this style of illiberal debate to a new low. The phenomenon of personal attack on people who expressed committed views in support of one side or another was something we could also have done without. Fortunately, partly as a result of technical incompetence, I have long since eschewed any desire to enter the alien world of social media, so I missed the excesses that apparently went on in cyberspace.

One strongly pro-independence thinker and a friend of mine even argued that one case for independence was to let clapped-out England float off to sink in its own mess. What a miserably selfish argument – I would argue that one reason for staying with the UK is precisely to give it the benefit of Scottish experience.

Scotland and the heritage of the United Kingdom

Scotland was the home of the Enlightenment. We had four universities for our small population when England had only two; in the fifteenth century King James IV gave us an Education Act, and we have John Knox and the Church of Scotland to thank for the establishment of a school in every parish; even today we leave the private sector to a small minority; the same is true of our national health service, unlike that of England.

In terms of explorers, missionaries, administrators, engineers and traders the Scots left their mark everywhere like the Jardines and Mathiesons in the far-east. Yet even those Scottish heroes of whom we are most proud were dependent on mutual support from English organisations whilst David Livingstone's remarkable exploits were on behalf of the London Missionary Society.

The same was true of the Scottish inventors. Sir Alexander Fleming developed the use of penicillin at St Mary's Hospital, London; James Watt his steam engines in Bristol and Cornwall; John Logie Baird his television in Hastings.

It is perhaps because part of my own upbringing was in Kenya that I am conscious of our huge influence in Africa. The former President of Zambia, Kenneth Kaunda, never tires of speaking warmly of his early education at a Scottish mission school in what was then Northern Rhodesia. He and many others saw that as an integral part of the UK's contribution to a developing world.

Scottish success in the administration of the UK and its interests are so strong that the story used to be told of the Scottish civil servant who was sent from St Andrew's House to undertake a familiarisation tour of Whitehall. On his return he was asked what he thought of the English, and he replied that he did not know, because he had only met heads of departments!

Scottish and British identity

So the referendum has been a divisive event, cutting across families, leading to harsh words, crossing political parties. Part of the reason is that it forced people to choose between an identity which is specifically Scottish and one in which Scottish and British identities can sit happily together. I personally believe this to be an unnecessary choice and that most people are, in varying degrees, Scottish, British, European – and, most importantly, Borderers, Glaswegians or Highlanders as the case may be.

Not long before the referendum campaign proper began, I attended the commemoration event of the life of Margo MacDonald and listened with great emotion to the tremendous eulogy to Margo delivered by her husband, Jim Sillars. It will undoubtedly stand as one of the greatest tributes of its kind, but the keynote was the plea from Margo that, the day after the referendum, whatever the result, people in Scotland should come together again, forgive the blows of the battle, heal the wounds and go forward united. This was an appeal taken up also by the Moderator of the Church of Scotland. Both of them spoke for many people.

New democratic opportunities

The other side of that coin has been the passion on both sides which has engaged many more people than any debate I can recall for many years. A high voter turnout, reversing the slow decline of many years in "normal" politics, lots of people on the doorsteps talking politics, well attended public meetings, a ferment of ideas around the referendum issues, strongly held views about the sort of country we want to live in – this has been the pattern for many months back in Scotland. A new sense of the importance of democratic debate all mixed up with the low abuse, spin and invective that have gone with democratic politics since the days of the Greeks and the Romans!

Liberal Democrats have always believed in the dynamism and idealism of young people as a spur to political action. One of the most pleasurable aspects of the referendum has been the more outward-looking views of younger people, influenced no doubt by social media and by global education, who see their lives against a much more international and pluralist – and hopefully Liberal – backdrop than did some previous generations.

Home Rule – more powers and entrenchment

The debate has slowly produced the beginnings of a national consensus which I believe will continue into the future.

On the Nationalist side, the First Minister and his strategists, forced to triangulate difficult issues, increasingly conceded the fundamental case for the United Kingdom – the pound, much macro-economic policy, the single UK economic market, the BBC, the NHS and even pensions, to say nothing of continuing co-operation on law and order, terrorism, Nato (despite its nuclear shield), defence and the use of overseas embassies.   They held themselves out as almost embarrassingly more Unionist than the Unionists. Changing the position of the Crown was a no go area in case it frightened the horses.   But their position was essentially a confederal one which envisaged continued collaboration across the United Kingdom in many areas.

But the pro-Union Parties also conceded the case for more powers, rounding off the Scottish Parliament's powers, particularly in terms of raising much more of its own taxation.   This is something which Liberal Democrats have always argued.   In my own Donald Dewar Memorial Lecture in 2003, I said that "no self respecting parliament can exist permanently on a grant from another parliament" – a theme developed in the report of the Steel Commission on "Moving to Federalism – A New Settlement for Scotland" in 2006[45] as well as in Ming Campbell's two later reports[46] for the Scottish Liberal Democrats.

Ming put it well in launching his Campbell 2 Report:

"Looking across Scotland's parties, it is clear that a consensus has formed around two broad propositions. Firstly, that the Scottish Parliament should raise the majority of what it spends.   Secondly, that the Scottish Parliament should be entrenched permanently."

---

[45] Steel Commission Report – "Moving to Federalism – A New Settlement for Scotland" March 2006 Scottish Liberal Democrats
[46] Campbell Commission Report – "Federalism – The best future for Scotland" October 2012 and Campbell 11 – "the Second Report of the Home Rule and Community Rule Commission" March 2014 Scottish Liberal Democrats

In terms of entrenchment, it was envisaged that there should be a resolution in both Holyrood and Westminster.

These changes would broadly complete the Scottish end of our Home Rule project and leave Scotland in a clear quasi-federal relationship to the rest of the United Kingdom. Interestingly this federal approach was what the Scottish Commissioners of Union wanted in 1705-6 (they were overborne by the English insistence on a single unitary Parliament).

If we look back to the events which led to the Union in 1707, the arguments are remarkably the same as those of today. The Darien scheme had been both a human and financial disaster, leading most people to the conclusion that competition and rivalry between England and Scotland was a wasteful luxury. The riots in the streets of Edinburgh did not occur when Union was proposed, and even Fletcher of Saltoun was in favour – it all went wrong with the proposed abolition of the Scottish Parliament, and we have now put that right, if not quite fully right.

"Home Rule all round" was envisaged by Gladstonian Liberals as the way forward after the achievement of Home Rule for Ireland. Home Rule was also the demand of the 1949 Scottish Covenant signed by two million out of Scotland's population of 5.1 million. The words of the Covenant are worth quoting:

"We, the people of Scotland who subscribe to this Engagement, declare our belief that reform in the constitution of our country is necessary to secure good government in accordance with our Scottish traditions and to promote the spiritual and economic welfare of our nation…

With that end in view we solemnly enter into this Covenant whereby we pledge ourselves, in all loyalty to the Crown and within the framework of the United Kingdom, to do everything in our power to secure for Scotland a Parliament with adequate legislative authority in Scottish affairs."

The need for UK federalism

So much for Scotland. It is very clear, however, that federalism has not yet breached the bastions of Westminster and Whitehall. In my view, that is something which requires to be remedied if, assuming a No vote in the current referendum, the future of the United Kingdom is to be assured. Failing significant change in UK structures, the independence issue could well come back to haunt us within a generation, just as Irish independence followed from the failure of Home Rule there over a century ago.

In the Steel Report, we commented that, although the Devolution project had bedded in remarkably smoothly, it remained a fractured project, lacking an overarching sense of purpose – "the mystery of the missing centre". We said that "no decentralised system has been conceived and operated with such little conscious attention to statewide co-ordination of government activity."[47]

That overarching sense of purpose is provided by federalism. With the benefit of hindsight, we can see the outlines of a new federal or quasi-federal structure for the United Kingdom beginning to emerge – a trend which has been given a powerful boost by the pressures released during the referendum debate.

What do we have to date?

- Scotland, Wales, Northern Ireland and, in a different way, London have the essential elements of Home Rule – domestic powers which have stood the test of time, growing fiscal responsibilities, the opportunity to do things differently to other parts of the United Kingdom.

---

[47] Steel Commission Report p20

- There are embryo federal institutions – the UK Supreme Court which has substantial constitutional powers; the joint Exchequer Committee provided for in the Scotland Act 2010 to look at new devolved taxes and other matters of tax effectiveness; the Bank of England – which is singularly misnamed but which is in practice the Reserve Bank of the United Kingdom; perhaps even a developing specialist role for HM Customs and Revenue.

- There are joint Ministerial Committees between Ministers of the home nations and UK Ministers – these have assumed some greater prominence with the arrival in power in Edinburgh in 2007 of a government of a different complexion to that in London.

- There is the British-Irish Council which was established in 1998 as a consequence of the Good Friday Agreement but which includes representatives of the devolved institutions, the Isle of Man and the Channel Islands and, "if appropriate of (devolved institutions) elsewhere in the United Kingdom".

These innovations at the UK level are far from minor developments but they are also part of a work in progress. They have also happened piecemeal – almost by accidental necessity – as a by-blow particularly of developments in Scotland.

UK Constitutional Convention?

Let me now turn to my main theme. Having co-chaired the Scottish Constitutional Convention (which devised the scheme for the Scottish Parliament) for almost a decade, I pay tribute to the patient and concrete work done in that body, which led to quick and positive action by the incoming Blair government in 1997.

I am not sure whether a carbon copy would work at UK level involving as it did almost all the local authorities in Scotland, as well as political parties, churches, trades unions and voluntary bodies, but a more compact constitutional convention or large commission is probably the best way forward – either as a mechanism to break some of the constitutional inertia which has developed at a UK level, or, in the unhappy event of a Yes vote in the referendum, to agree how to order the many things that would benefit from common UK decision-making.

Alan Riley, the professor of law at City University, has advanced an intriguing additional argument for us to head in the direction of a written constitution, namely protection against mission creep from Brussels which so exercises politicians and press alike. He writes:

"A British version would, like the German Basic Law, set out the major institutions of the state, set out principles and enumerate fundamental rights. The British Supreme Court would then be able to police the borders of the EU's jurisdiction in a similar fashion to the German courts".

But my main concern in promoting the same idea is to bring some cohesion and principle to the developing governance of the United Kingdom.

For the truth is that all of our recent institutions including the Scottish and European Parliaments have just grown up higgedly-piggedly along with other legislation dealing with the rights of our citizens, such as the European Convention on Human Rights and Freedom of Information. Whilst I can understand how this happened we need to question whether constitutional reform should always be done on such an *ad hoc* basis.

We need a clear understanding of why and where powers lie. Federal countries have the benefit of written and codified arrangements. We have written arrangements but they are of varying standards and clarity. They are not all in one place, and they invariably are written arrangements to suit the centre. They are not about the constitutional protection of the nations or indeed their peoples and their rights.

Federalism is now attracting the support of leading figures across Britain – including former Prime Ministers Sir John Major and Gordon Brown as well as academics, lawyers and influential thinkers like David Melding, a Welsh Conservative AM, who has called for a new Treaty of Union presaged by a Declaration of Federal Union.

Gordon Brown has even written a book on the subject[48] in which he sets out his belief that Scots need to have confidence in the benefits of a UK-wide union, or "covenant between nations", guaranteeing social and economic rights, among them pensions, unemployment assistance, fully funded healthcare and minimum standards at work, including the minimum wage. A union "based simply on the crown, the pound, the military or Team GB is not, in the end, as democratic or as emotionally valid as a union of common social interests between and among peoples and nations."

Gordon Brown envisages a New United Kingdom as a network of partnership obligations between the different nations and Westminster. He also now supports House of Lords reform as a means towards entrenching the rights of the nations and regions – a proposition which I and other Liberal Democrats have advanced for many years.

An Elephant in the Room – the English problem
The distinguished Scottish-born, but London-based, political journalist Neil Ascherson, himself once a candidate for the Scottish Parliament in the Liberal Democrat interest, is an expert on the politics of Eastern Europe. He was greatly excerised about what he described as "the elephant in the room" – by which he meant what to do about the

---

[48] Gordon Brown - "My Scotland, Our Britain – A Future Worth Sharing" June 2014 Simon & Schuster Ltd.

governance of England in a reformed, federal United Kingdom. England, of course, comprises around 85% of the population of the UK.

The Liberal Democrats, essentially and traditionally supporters of devolution from Whitehall to the great Regions of England, now back a programme of devolution on demand for the regions, envisaging that this process might unlock the box of English decentralisation starting probably in Cornwall (with its strong Celtic heritage, language and history) and Yorkshire.

Some people support an English Parliament as a federal unit, equivalent to Scotland, Wales and Northern Ireland. Still others have suggested an England based on city-regions. Perhaps England needs to devolve into city states like London but with a rural hinterland. This is a matter for decision in England but I can't help thinking, firstly, that a single English federal unit would be so large as to destabilise the United Kingdom but secondly that ways need to be found of accommodating the sense of all-England identity within its governance. Squaring that circle is undoubtedly a big challenge but one that can no longer be put off by the majority of us who value a strong United Kingdom.

The Purpose of the United Kingdom

But constitutional navel-gazing is ultimately less important than sentiment and substance. The United Kingdom will endure because its people have a common sentiment and interest in its continuance and in its contemporary purpose.

The long drawn out debate on independence has distracted the Scottish government from giving priority to deep-rooted problems in Scotland such as the pervading poverty and unemployment disfiguring so many of our public housing estates, and the existence of what the late Ralf Dahrendorf called an underclass. In similar fashion, the hostile and sterile obsession with Europe that has dominated much political discourse at UK level, particularly on the right, has been a distraction from more substantial issues.

Our political arguments today tend to be mainly about money with very little reference to collective purpose, taste or culture. Beveridge in his day just took for granted a high level of public moral agreement and civic awareness. He assumed that social cohesion was not just desirable but essential. Solidarity with our fellow citizens was the underlying motivation for his famous Report, and he believed politicians should search for agreement rather than conflict.

The need for a written constitution for the United Kingdom has been developed by Robert Brown in his essay. Here I simply observe that I believe that such a constitution, as well as laying down the structures of government, the relationships between the Federal institutions and the nations and regions of the United Kingdom and the traditional freedoms, should also place a new emphasis on achieving social justice and opportunity, a new determination to tackle the entrenched problems of poverty and multiple deprivation and give a new importance to the ethos that should animate public institutions, business corporations and the media. It was, after all, the failure of so many of the elites in recent years which led to the crisis of confidence in our democratic institutions.

A final challenge to the purpose, cohesion and integrity of the United Kingdom comes from the dominance of London. London is a great global city and a huge asset to our country – but its sheer size, scale and economic predominance are also a challenge to the rest of the country. How we balance and offset London's pre-eminence, how we enhance the powers and standing of our great regional cities may well determine the social health and balance of the whole United Kingdom in the future.

A United Kingdom Senate

One of the key tasks of a UK Constitutional Convention could be how to organise a more genuinely federal-type style of government throughout the United Kingdom. Here is where the reform of the House of Lords to create a more useful and democratic institution comes into play.

Unfortunately the authors of the most recent attempt at Lords reform by the coalition government either ignored – or possibly were ignorant of – the history of the subject. Their bill predictably foundered in the House of Commons on the arguments of MPs against creating a second elected Chamber which could threaten the supremacy of the House of Commons. Some were also rightly concerned at the thought of senators (elected for fifteen years) wandering around and meddling in their constituencies.

Prime Minister Asquith in his preface to the Parliament Act of 1911 was careful not to use the word "elected" when promising future reforms. What he actually said was: "It is intended to substitute for the House of Lords as it at present exists a Second Chamber constituted on a popular instead of hereditary basis".

He appointed a high powered commission under Viscount Bryce to take this forward. In 1918 it recommended a second chamber largely elected by MPs on a regional basis, and their report stated: "it was forcibly argued that a Chamber elected on the same franchise as the House of Commons would inevitably become a rival".

The post-war Labour government of Mr Atlee initiated all party talks which at least reached tentative agreement that a reformed Upper House "should be complementary to and not a rival to" the lower House. The coalition government blithely ignored all these long-standing conclusions and expressed indignation when their inadequate bill, as was wholly foreseeable, hit the buffers.

As Liberal leader, I myself consistently called for the second Chamber to include representatives of the nations and regions of the United Kingdom – from my first general election manifesto as Liberal Party leader in 1979 to my last election as Alliance party leader in 1987 jointly with David Owen.

All three parties are now considering what to put into their next manifesto on the subject of Lords reform. I just hope they have learned from the recent fiasco, and in the spirit of helpfulness I offer my own suggestions on what such a new Upper Chamber might look like and what it could do.

A Senate of around 500 members would be significantly fewer than the 650 Members of the Commons, and well below our current 830 peers.

Around 300 could be elected for England by MPs and MEPs regionally, 32 by MSPs, MEPs and MPs in Scotland, 20 similarly by the Welsh and 12 from Northern Ireland – all by proportional representation.

A further 100 cross benchers could be chosen by the same electorate but excluding anyone who was or had recently been a member of any political party. These would replace the existing valuable wide range of independent expertise we have at present on the cross benches in the Lords. The fact that the cross-benchers – with their wide range of independent and distinguished expertise from outside life – are a 25% bloc in our Chamber prevents any government from having a built-in majority in the Lords. I would also like to add to the federal flavour by giving one seat to each of the Crown Dependencies – Jersey, Guernsey & the Isle of Man. A convention could develop where in the Upper House each section did not vote on matters which did not apply to their territory, thus partially answering the unanswerable West Lothian question.

101

The powers of a reformed Upper House would remain as at present – no veto, only delay, and the right to ask the Commons to think again, and no power over finance.

The Scottish Parliament might like to consider whether the Scottish thirty-two in such a reformed House could not also act as a long-stop for them. Post-legislative scrutiny does not exist at Holyrood and here could be a useful and inexpensive way of providing it.

The Style of Politics

A radical programme of democratic renewal in the United Kingdom cannot escape the issue of the style of our politics. Politics has always been robust but, at its best, it is also principled, passionate, able to engage the public, and an articulation of great causes.

No one can say that Prime Minister's Question Time – which should capture these things as one of Parliament's big, dramatic occasions – is an advert for democracy. It is no longer Prime Minister's Question Time – it has become Prime Minister's Insult Time with the two protagonists exchanging well-rehearsed sound bites.

Fortunately that loss of proper scrutiny of government has been offset by the growth in power and influence of the departmental select committees who haul ministers and public officials before them for interrogation.

But sadly the same adverse trend in the Chamber itself has set in at Holyrood, though at the start we decided on a semi-circular chamber rather than one where opposing parties sat two carefully measured swords' lengths apart. Under the benign leadership of Donald Dewar that seemed to work for the first few years, but no longer – belligerence and stridency are the order of the day and too many have forgotten the prime duty of holding the Executive to account.

This is partly because one party now has an over-all majority which was never the intention of the original legislation introducing proportional representation.

Turning back to the House of Commons I am struck by how much it has changed drastically since I appeared in 1965 as baby of the House. When I arrived there were captains of industry, major trade union leaders, chairmen of banks, miners, service chiefs, steel workers and people in senior positions in a range of professions. That has all changed.

The common route into parliament has become the same in all parties – you work as researcher to an MP or at party headquarters or serve your party on your local council.

Selection committees no longer ask "who would be our best MP?" but "who deserves our party's nomination as candidate?" I applauded David Cameron's initiative in suggesting open primaries – and these have thrown up a few interesting people out of the standard mould, but they are rare exceptions.

In fairness I should note two improvements in the composition of the Commons – the advent of many more women (a rise from about a dozen to 143) and the reduction in numbers of the very elderly thanks to the introduction of parliamentary pensions.

The increasing role of spin doctors is to be deplored. They hand out questions for MPs to ask, and they daily bombard party activists by email with "lines to take" – not least on the alleged achievements of the LibDems in the coalition government. The latest additions to these daily outpourings are suggested tweets to circulate. Fortunately I am not a tweeter, so I swiftly delete all these unread. All of this contributes to the diminution of individual expression or even thought in politics. Little wonder that the paid-up membership of political parties is in decline.

Conclusion

The dust of the Scottish independence referendum is settling, the acres of print devoted to the issue has diminished, the international journalists have decamped elsewhere. My contention in this essay has been that the nations of Britain, whatever the outcome of the referendum, will have to move on to create a more modern pattern of governance in these islands, fit for the challenges of the current age but which nevertheless build on 300 years of a common polity.

It is in that spirit that I have put forward these suggestions for a constructive way forward in the governance of our disparate, attractive and I hope continuing United Kingdom. We could do worse than put at the centre of our common endeavours the words of the great South African author and campaigner Alan Paton who wrote:

"By Liberalism I do not mean the creed of any party or any century. I mean a generosity of spirit, a tolerance of others, a commitment to the rule of law, a high ideal of the worth and dignity of man, a repugnance of authoritarianism and a love of freedom".

Quo vadis Europa?

Graham Watson

Where is Europe heading? And what is Scotland's and Britain's rightful place within it? The SNP's shenanigans in 2013-14 bring such questions to the fore. Liberal Democrats must have convincing answers.

If ever the European Union had to prove its worth, 2008 was the moment. The twin global financial crises of unsustainable sovereign debt and insufficient bank capitalisation were brutally exposed by the collapse of Lehman Brothers. Scotland's largest bank, RBS, was left spinning in the maelstrom released by the crash. Such was the extent of the UK Prime Minister's toadying to Rupert Murdoch that British newspaper headlines screamed 'Gordon Brown saves the world'. The sober reality is that swift action by the US Federal Reserve and the European Central Bank (followed Fido-like by Northern-Rock-frightened Britain) prevented a near disaster from becoming a catastrophe.

The courage and the deep pockets of ECB Governor Jean Claude Trichet allowed a central bank which was less than a decade old to keep afloat the seventeen countries of the Euro-zone and some beyond. Without his injection onto financial markets of billions of euros in liquidity over four crucial nights in September 2008, whole countries would have been bankrupted and banks brought crashing down. Imagine the situation that week if the ECB had not pooled and built on (and been able to call on without delay) the eurozone's reserves; and if Europe had still traded in drachmas, escudos, pesetas, lire and punts! The EU would have been smashed to smithereens as national parliaments clutched at atavistic policies of nationalisation and exchange controls. Efficient and timely co-ordination of so many different national currencies would have been impossible.

Britain's decision in 1997 not to join the euro (more accurately, the setting of conditions for UK membership by Chancellor Gordon Brown which could not conceivably be fulfilled) had relegated the UK to the sidelines long before the crash. Moreover the UK economy, sustained by a lethal cocktail of inflated house prices, cavalier consumer credit, casinos and drink, was in little better shape than that of Italy and paled beside the German giant. And though Brown and Cameron declared that we would not take part in Europe's bailout of Greece, they kept mighty quiet about how we participated instead, to about the same amount, in the US arm of the bailout through the IMF. Even today, the idea that the UK economy is somehow in great shape while the euro has brought ruin on those who joined defies serious analysis. It is another euro-myth.

The UK has a clear choice in Europe, exposed then as much as now. We can have either independence or influence, but not both. The more we sacrifice our independence, the more influence we gain. Our decision not to join the euro (which has now grown from 12 to 18 countries, soon to be 19) and our decision to stay out of the EU's banking union have meant we have precious little say in the major decisions on our continent. This matters less in good times; Greece is now back on its feet with its budget in surplus (though recovery for Greece and others, as for Britain, is fitful). It is hugely important in times of trouble.

A country clinging to its own currency cannot count on the same solidarity as a eurozone member.

Building the political conditions for membership of the eurozone is thus a crucial task for Liberal Democrats. The arguments must be about influence (or the lack of influence outside the eurozone, where the Chancellor of the Exchequer is invited to join his euro-zone counterparts at the EU's fortnightly Council of Finance Ministers only after they have agreed the most important matters between themselves) and about security. In times of turbulence the ping-pong ball of sterling will be bounced back and forth between the basketballs of the dollar and the euro. Some independence!

Is the EU democratic?

Since the Lisbon Treaty the European Union has enjoyed a truly bicameral legislature, with an executive under the watchful eyes of two chambers and with everyone subject to the European Court of Justice (not to be confused, please, with the European Court of Human Rights in Strasbourg, much as Liberals should admire both). True, the first chamber – the Council – consists of *indirectly* elected heads of state and government and their government ministers. This chamber has the right of initiative in policy making, a right which it delegates in certain instances to the executive branch, the European Commission. The European Parliament – as the second chamber, the equivalent of the UK's House of Lords – has no formal right of initiative. But, unlike the UK's second chamber, the European Parliament is democratically elected, its members voted in by the ballots of the European Union's citizens. Sadly, turnout at European elections (though it rose slightly in 2014) suggests the voters are largely unaware of its powers.

Does the participation at elections of fewer than 50% of those entitled to vote suggest a deficit in democracy? If so, should we not discuss the 'democratic deficit' in UK local government or the 'democratic deficit' in US Presidential elections? Liberal Democrats could convincingly argue for voting to be made compulsory, as in Belgium or Australia; we should argue for the right of citizens to vote electronically. We should not fall into the UKIP trap of suggesting that the EU is less valid because many of its electors choose not to vote.

An area in which much progress has been made to reduce a former democratic deficit is that of law-making. The European Parliament, with very few and well-justified exceptions, invariably meets in public session in all its legislative instances. Until recently the EU's Council of Ministers did not. A campaign by Liberal Democrat MEPs under their 2002-09 leader successfully strong-armed the European Council formations into webstreaming most of their sessions, though the heads of state and government themselves have managed to remain partially largely aloof from this.

A similar campaign is needed now by Liberal Democrat MEPs to rectify the major area where a democratic deficit still arises: the lack of openness or transparency in decision making. The Access to Documents legislation (Article 255 Regulation of 2001) has never been properly implemented. Member states frequently lodge documents with the Commission only on condition that these are not made public. And since sunlight is the best disinfectant, germs can fester in its absence. A campaign is now needed to ensure compliance with Article 255 of the Treaties. Were it to succeed, it would provide freedom of information laws better than those enjoyed by citizens in most of the EU's member states, while still giving those who govern us 'space to think'.

Scrutiny of executive appointments and decisions in Brussels is now better than in many member states. But of course that scrutiny is exercised by fewer elected members, further away. And if the alarming tendency of broadsheets to devote more space to the lives of celebrities than to the affairs of the world is followed almost slavishly by a BBC which rides roughshod over its duty to educate and to inform, few can wonder that democracy is damaged. Holyrood and Westminster are finally catching up with Scandinavian parliaments in improving national scrutiny of EU governance, but few citizens ever learn about their deliberations.

In this sense the debate about *Spitzenkandidaten*, the lead candidates for each of the political groups in the European Parliament, (and their corollary, voting in EP elections for supranational rather than national lists of candidates) is instructive. What Cameron really objected to about Juncker is that he was elected by the European People's Party, from which the Tories withdrew in 2009. (Had they stayed, their votes might have ensured that Michel Barnier, much more to the Tories' liking, beat Juncker in the EPP's selection contest.) Similarly, Schulz was elected by the Socialists and would have run the Commission if they had won the election. The EU's Liberal Democrats, and the Greens and the far Left, also chose lead candidates by the same procedure which made Cameron first Conservative Party leader and then PM. Only the European Conservative and Reform Party, the one to which Cameron belongs, decided not to elect a candidate for Commission President; they preferred to take their wickets home. In the USA, which most Conservatives consider a democracy, the major political parties come together at Union level every four years to select and campaign for a Presidential hopeful; that the same happens in the post-Lisbon EU should not be seen as revolutionary. That the process now happens almost entirely in the English language (though German is the EU's most widely spoken mother tongue by far) should not make UK Conservatives feel less comfortable.

The first refuge of every elected scoundrel is to blame another tier of government for social ills. In Ayrshire, blame Edinburgh; in Holyrood, blame Whitehall and so on. The problem with bashing Brussels from Friday to Wednesday (while claiming the credit yourself for all its successes) is that few will then vote for it on Thursday. The election of a UKIP MEP in Scotland shows this problem is not confined to England. But is 'Brussels' bad? The truth is that Brussels is a chimera. There is no *deus ex machina*. There are civil servants recruited from 28 member states reporting to MEPs elected from 28 member states and Ministers appointed by 28 member states. *The fault, dear Brutus, lies not in our stars but in our selves ...*

The hosting in Scotland of the Commonwealth Games rather than (say) the European Football Championships led some to focus on yesterday's benefits of Empire accrued through Union with England and Wales, rather than today's benefits of EU membership. The concentration in the second edition of *'Homecoming'* on the New World rather than the old exaggerates this head-in-the-sand nostalgia. Yet the number of present-day (rather than umpteenth generation) Scots living and working on the continent of Europe gives a more tangible taste of the realities of modern Scotland. In Germany, one of the most prominent politicians of the CDU is a Scot; a prominent historian at the University of Tuebingen too. The Scotland which bequeathed to Europe the philosophy of David Hume, the economic insights of Adam Smith, scientists from Watt to Geddes and writers from Duns Scotus to Alasdair Gray need not lack the self confidence to find its own place in the European Union of today. More populous, more prosperous and more productive than half the current member states of the EU, to embrace a wider concept of the democratic polity could well pay dividends.

Should the EU have a foreign policy?

Since the Lisbon Treaty, it has. In every third country it is now the EU representation which takes the lead, convening the diplomatic representatives of the member states on a regular basis and representing them collectively. As a result there is now hardly a national diplomat who would not prefer to be in the EU's European External Action Service or EEAS. (Many already are, since the service has recruited mainly from its member state foreign offices; many more apply every time an EU post is advertised.) The foreign ministers of the member states meet in Council on a regular basis; they set policy together. Is this surprising? No. Prior to the formation of the EEAS, no EU member state any longer had an embassy in every third country, for reasons of cost. Only the UK and Germany had representations in more than two thirds of them. With the development of the EEAS and the pressure to reduce national government deficits, expect more to close. Any EU citizen can seek help from an EU diplomatic representation or from that of any other member state. Moreover, there are now over twenty EU military, police or peacekeeping missions around the world, from Palestine to Indonesia. Individual member states can no longer afford them, and where the Americans do not wish to intervene, NATO cannot.

You missed these developments? Blame the UK media! It was after all under a European Commissioner from the UK, Baroness Ashton, (the EU's High Representative for Foreign and Security Policy), that the EEAS has been built.

Is the EU committed to sustainability?

Were it not for the EU, there would be no Kyoto Protocol. The drive by Brussels for supranational and intercontinental agreements to combat climate change has been relentless. Of course it has been helped by the de-industrialisation of Europe's economy; or, perhaps more accurately, the process of globalisation which has moved labour intensive manufacturing processes to places where labour is less expensive. Yet the European Climate Foundation's groundbreaking *Roadmap 2050* project, which inspired the European Commission's low carbon roadmap and has led to the setting by Council and Parliament of ambitious targets for environmental sustainability based on a switch from hydrocarbons to low carbon energy sources, has changed to parameters of debate. Liberal Democrats will have to learn to live with (if not to love) nuclear energy, which is central to meeting energy demand while making the green energy switch; in the process it could save us from the perils of fracking. Since the scientists tell us that two thirds of all the world's known oil and gas deposits must stay in the ground if we are to limit average temperature rises to 2°C in this century, this is not rocket-science for environmentalists like we Liberal Democrats. Recent moves by the UK and Poland to renationalise energy policy must not be allowed to stand in the way of the EU meeting its climate commitments or indeed setting more ambitious commitments in the forthcoming UNFCCC.

Is the EU Liberal?

A truly remarkable feature of the EU remains the tendency of its leaders to think more generously at EU level than they do at home. While nationally they seek to restrict migration, to offer a less generous welcome to those seeking asylum, to act tough on law and order and to pretend that the military-industrial nation state can meet all the needs of its citizens, at EU level they recognise their international obligations and appear to know instinctively that to face the big global challenges they need to pool their sovereignty. The challenge of survival and prosperity in an increasingly global economy, the challenges of rising world population growth and migration, of climate change and energy security, of protecting their citizens from internationally organised crime ... all these become clear when ministers or MEPs discuss common responses to common questions beyond the thought-bubbles of their national capitals. Open trading relationships and the competition and other legal regimes which facilitate them seem self-evident. Common solutions emerge to common challenges. Similarly, shared investments in the exploration of space or in other areas of technology, in military hardware for civilian uses and in applied scientific research capture the imagination (and relieve the pockets) of national governments co-operating at EU level.

Yet at the very top level, leadership has been lamentable. The Liberal agendas pursued by Roy Jenkins and Gaston Thorn or the social democratic sense of Jacques Delors are long gone. The European People's Party dominates the politics of the continent with a mixture of broadly benevolent northern European christian democracy and the corrupt obscenity of Silvio Berlusconi, Traian Basescu or Viktor Orban. Over two decades, successive Commission Presidents have allowed the EU to be pushed around by the larger member states. The leaders of some of those member states seek precisely that kind of Commission President. Liberals must not let them.

Liberal Democrats in the EP have successfully insisted on more women in the top jobs, on parliamentary approval of those holding public office, on scrutiny of the actions of those taking decisions. Liberal Democrat MEPs, like George Lyon when he was Vice Chair of the Budget Committee, have worked hard to ensure value for money for the taxpayer. This reform agenda must be pursued vigourously. The answer may be less Europe in some areas, more in others. But it is vital to be in it to win it. That understanding escapes the parties of the right and is insufficiently inculcated in the left. Liberal Democrats must remain in the vanguard.

Human Rights under Challenge

Robert Brown

One of the more important side products of both the Scottish referendum and the debate around the future of Europe has been a renewed interest in written constitutions, the nature of fundamental liberties and the place of human rights in our law. Recently too the Commons' Political Reform Committee has indicated that the 800th anniversary of Magna Carta is a good time to look again at the issue of a written constitution.

It is perhaps worth saying that one of the greatest things we can say about the United Kingdom is that it was the first country to produce a Parliamentary and court system which had at its heart the protection of civil and political liberties. This came out of struggle and civil war, revolution and social change – against the Church, against the Crown, against the government, with many setbacks and many anomalies – and it was based on that key element which the constitutional writers used to describe as "the spirit of a free people". This was a tremendous achievement, and one not to be disparaged when, in the excesses of the recent referendum campaign, the Yes campaign disparaged the United Kingdom and asked its purpose, or when UKIP-minded people disparage the

European Convention on Human Rights to which Britain made such a signal contribution.

That sense of civil liberty and of fair play in the UK remains a huge asset. It is still there to be tapped into but it cannot be taken for granted. It has to be fought for anew in each generation and Liberals should be the leading champions of it.

Written constitution

The United Kingdom famously – along with Israel and New Zealand – has no written constitution. This was never entirely true since the English and Scottish Acts of Union of 1706 are clearly constitutional documents – as are the Act of Settlement of 1701, the Parliament Acts of 1911 and 1949 and various other pieces of legislation. More recently, the European Communities Act 1972, the Scotland Acts1997 and 2010, the Human Rights Act 1997 and the Fixed Term Parliament Act 2011 are clearly all legislation of a constitutional nature. Added together, legislation like this comprises a significant body of constitutional law.

But does it have a constitutional status? The theory of Parliamentary sovereignty as defined by Dicey states that no Parliament can bind its successor. Parliament, he said, has the right to make or unmake any law whatever and there is no person or body recognised by the law as having a right to override or set aside the legislation of Parliament. However, since at least the Statute of Westminster of 1931 conferring independence on the British Dominions, this has been a polite fiction at best in the realm of public international law. The United Kingdom Parliament could no doubt in theory rescind the independence of Australia or even the United States, and such a law might be recognised by our courts, but this is an area where the realities of politics supersede legal theory.

The status of the Scottish Parliament and the Welsh Assembly is rather different. Despite the Sewell convention that Westminster will not legislate in a devolved area without the consent of the Scottish Parliament, there is no formal constitutional protection for the devolved institutions. And there is a precedent – in the abolition of the previous Stormont Parliament set up in 1920 as a result of the Troubles.

But the Scottish Parliament and the Welsh and Northern Ireland Assemblies were reinforced by the backing of referenda, so political reality also dictates that they would not be abolished unilaterally by Westminster. The 1997 referendum underpinned the Scottish Parliament; in turn, this gained authority from the inclusive process of the Scottish Constitutional Convention; it has been followed in spirit by the Edinburgh Agreement which gives legality to the recent independence referendum.

The position of the European Union is similar. Westminster gave the European institutions both specific and general jurisdiction in Treaty areas including the right in certain circumstances to override even a UK Act of Parliament. This too was approved by a referendum (although many people argue that the major changes such as the Maastricht Treaty which have since taken place weakens the force of that referendum). Technically we could leave the EU, as UKIP and some Conservatives wish to do. In practice, this would now amount to a major revolution.

So the existence of constitutional entities which have been entrenched by referenda is pretty secure. However the same is not necessarily true for other constitutional laws such as the Human Rights Act, or indeed the Crown Proceedings Act which secured the right of the citizen to sue the government for breach of the law. Nor does the existence or status of Local Government have protection under UK law. Again, the practice may be rather different:

withdrawing from the ECHR would wreak havoc in our law which has increasingly seen human rights principles as fundamental to the legal system. Liberal Democrats, to their great credit in the current UK Parliament, have stopped Conservative vandals tearing up the ECHR. There is an odd similarity between Tony Blair's hamfisted moves to abolish the position of Lord Chancellor and the Tory attacks on human rights. The trouble is that neither of them understood the fundamental principles of what they were doing in the first place.

But the conclusion must be that it is high time that the affairs both of Scotland and of the United Kingdom, as David Steel argues in his essay, should have the constitutional protection of a written constitution which would both define the powers of the institutions of a more federal country and entrench key civil and human rights protections beyond the reach of government. For Liberal Democrats certainly and for many others, there is a "law of nations", a charter of human rights and principles, a "natural law" that sits above the sovereignty of Parliament and should be able to hold the acts of Parliaments and Governments accountable if they do not conform to this standard.

The Campbell Commission report[49], whose principles have been approved both by the Scottish Liberal Democrats and by the Federal Liberal Democrat Conference, set out a route map to home rule and federalism; its second part argued the case for community power; but, throughout, the Commission report viewed federalism and the written constitution it implied as being the optimum way to limit the power of government and enhance the power of the citizen. The Liberal Democrat Federal Conference in York in March

---

[49] Federalism: the best future for Scotland – Report of a Commission chaired by Sir Menzies Campbell QC, MP October 2012 Scottish Liberal Democrats

2014[50] called for the establishment of a constitutional convention to draw up a written federal constitution for the United Kingdom. Federalism is, in essence, much more sympathetic to human rights than a unitary form of government based on the doctrine of the sovereignty of Parliament – which is ultimately a most illiberal doctrine.

Importance of human rights in Britain

But many people would argue that the threat to human rights in the United Kingdom is small beer compared to the abuses and threats to life, limb and property experienced by people in other parts of the world.

No doubt the threat to civil liberties in Britain is not of the level seen in Iraq with the summary execution of opponents of the Islamic State's Caliphate, in Egypt with the arrest of Al Jazeera journalists or in South Africa under apartheid. But, despite the incorporation of the European Convention on Human Rights into domestic law by the Human Rights Act 1998, a Report by the Equality and Human Rights Commission in 2008 found that, even in largely benign public bodies in Britain, a culture of respect for human rights has largely failed to take root among public authorities in England, Scotland and Wales in the way that was anticipated when the Human Rights Act was passed. The Reporter commented:

I think an organisation that has an embedded human rights culture and processes is something like a yeti – we know what it might look like and we've heard it might exist but we've certainly never seen one!

Rights are secured in a variety of ways – by courts, by Government action to provide services, by Parliaments passing good laws, but above all by respect for civil liberties as an intrinsic part of political and civic culture and ethos. At

---

[50] Resolution on "Power to the People" – York Conference March 2014

all these levels, and even more so in the ordinary practice of government, bureaucracy and corporate activity, human rights understanding needs to be at the heart of things if citizens – and indeed non-citizens – are to have their rights secured.

Human rights in Scotland

So where do we stand at the moment? What is the standing of human rights at home in Scotland?

Firstly, in the institutional sense, the work of the two Human Rights Commissions – the SCHR and the EHRC – has made an impressive contribution. When, as a Liberal Democrat Minister, I took the Bill to establish the SCHR through the Scottish Parliament, it had something of a torrid time. People like the SNP's John Swinney claimed it was unnecessary, there was no gap to fill, it was a waste of money. I am not sure if Mr. Swinney has changed his mind on this but I concede that the current Scottish government has at least not moved to abolish the Commission.

However there are major human rights causes to be defended. The challenges made by Liberal Democrat Justice spokesperson, Alison McInnes MSP, to the centralisation of the police, the use of firearms by the police in the Highlands and the extended use of stop and search tactics on children – have all illustrated the somewhat cavalier attitude to these matters under the current Scottish government – and they followed the curious approach by the Justice Secretary to various other matters – his Pontius Pilate attitude to the use of tasers by the police, and his trampling on proper procedures in the Lockerbie bomber case. A recent issue has been the failure of the SNP government to provide sufficient resources to support rehabilitation of prisoners[51] – a key issue

---

[51] SNP have dropped the ball on prison rehabilitation – Scottish Liberal Democrats Press Release – 11th July 2014 – revealed that

both for prisoners and, at least as importantly, for their victims.

The Scottish Government is currently intent, despite protest from almost everyone who knows anything about it, on abolishing the longstanding law on corroboration in Scotland. And that in turn follows their highly defensive attitude when the UK Supreme Court overthrew long standing practices relating to arrest and detention in the Cadder case[52] as being non compliant with ECHR – and were blasted by the Justice Secretary and by the First Minister in terms I do not recall being used by governments to courts in any western country. Maybe Mr. Berlusconi in Italy said similar things. In any event, the Scottish Government had to rush through much criticised emergency legislation to deal with the verdict.

It is also hugely disappointing that the SNP Government seem to have no real sense that a balanced constitution which safeguards human rights needs to have some checks and balances on government – certainly constitutional entrenchment of the independent mandate of local government, perhaps a revising Chamber, perhaps an enhanced majority to change what they themselves regard as a constitutional law, perhaps a Human Rights Committee which the Scottish Parliament, unlike Westminster, noticeably lacks. It certainly did not suggest a changed regime when the SNP, in its pre-referendum manifesto (the so-called 'White Paper") blithely confirmed its intention to take over the Crown's prerogative powers unchanged – these are the real powers now exercised by the Government, not the theoretical ones left to the Queen. Given how long they had had to prepare, it is astonishing how embryonic was the SNP offering on these things.

---

almost 1,000 inmates had been placed on waiting lists in Scottish prisons for programmes designed to reduce offending
[52] Cadder v HMA 2010 UKSC 43

UK government and human rights

But the United Kingdom government too, despite the presence of Liberal Democrat Ministers in the Coalition, has had its own travails over human rights. We began well by getting rid of Labour's ID cards and we saw off the Conservative attempts to get rid of the ECHR under the guise of a British Bill of Rights[53]. We have found, though, that control orders under Labour's Prevention of Terrorism Act 2005, immigration controls and deportations, "secret" courts and a variety of issues associated with surveillance give us rather more problems. Even our success in blocking the Communications Data Bill (the "Snooper's Charter") in 2013 leaves a whole raft of legacy issues which arose again in July 2014 when the UK Government announced emergency legislation[54] to allow them to continue to require phone companies to store emails and phone calls for 12 months. The Bill, required to get round a European Court of Justice decision striking down the (EU) European Date Retention Directive, is subject to significant restrictions secured by Liberal Democrats including a sunset clause (in 2016), and is accompanied by a wide ranging Review of legislation allowing public bodies to access private communications. Nevertheless, as in Scotland, emergency legislation seldom enhances human rights and is seldom as urgent as claimed by Governments.

The Party gave a stern and valid warning on this issue at its Spring Conference: "Indiscriminate harvesting and storage of the communications and metadata of people without suspicion is incompatible with our liberal and

---

[53] A British Bill of Rights which builds on rather than neuters the ECHR has long been a Liberal Democrat policy objective
[54] The Data Retention and Investigation Powers Bill 2014

democratic principles, and has the potential to cast a chilling effect on free speech and free association."[55]

Balancing essential human rights with effective action and protection against terrorists is pretty tricky but, as Liberty pointed out[56], the invidious idea of a "war on terror" can mean that "rights, freedoms and the rule of law are fatally compromised in a permanent state of emergency". This framework of fundamental rights and freedoms is what distinguishes us from both tyrants and terrorists.

I mention these things to make the point that all Governments, within their respective jurisdictions, are capable of playing ducks and drakes with human rights, and that it is political and civic attitudes rather than national structures which are the key determinant of the defence of civil liberties.

Interestingly the principal criticisms of the courts recently have tended to come from the right wing – not least in terrorism cases. Both the Labour government and the current Home Secretary have run into issues in this area and have been sent home to think again. Fortunately, there is a prevailing judicial view that, even in difficult times, governments are not entitled to arrest, detain or imprison people, even with the most appalling attitudes or actions alleged against them, without due process of law and in accordance both with domestic law and with widely accepted international norms enforced through the jurisprudence of the ECHR and other human rights concords.

I take the view that the role of the courts is to do justice according to the law, that part of the role involves the

---

[55] Motion F19 on "A Digital Bill of Rights" – Liberal Democrats' Spring Conference, York – March 2014
[56] "From War to Law" – Liberty's Response to the Coalition Government's Review of Counter-Terrorism and Security Powers 2010

protection of the citizen – and indeed the non-citizen – against arbitrary excesses of government power, and that the courts rightly and increasingly have a new role in the UK which is to uphold the rules of the constitution.

The United Kingdom Supreme Court is explicitly able to opine on devolution questions which in effect decide the constitutional legality of Scottish Parliament legislation and the human rights compliance of criminal procedure. But increasingly the idea of the sovereignty of the UK Parliament is being replaced by a new balance under which acts of the Government and the legislation of Parliaments operates "within the constitution" and is subject to being struck down by the courts using the weapon of judicial review and the framework of the ECHR. Incidentally, if you think that modern Parliaments have occasionally had their disreputable moments, can I mention that the Scots Parliament of 1661 (not one particularly concerned with human rights) was referred to as "the Drunken Parliament" on the basis that its members were almost perpetually drunk!

Action needed on Human Rights

Human rights are not sufficiently defended by either Parliament or the courts. This is why the SHRC believes that Scotland "needs a more systematic approach to assure and not assume the realisation of human rights in practice" and why they developed Scotland's National Action Plan for Human Rights[57].

Cases only come before the courts if citizens are prepared to bring them, lawyers are prepared to fight them and there is an affordable structure of justice to facilitate it. The options have been widened by the introduction of various forms of Tribunal, of Ombudsmen and Commissioners of various kinds, and more broadly by the development of administrative law procedures. Rightly, these offices are

---

[57] December 2013

normally subject to appointment by the Scottish Parliament and, less frequently, by the UK Parliament rather than by the Government but unfortunately they are sometimes themselves characterised by obscurity, delay, circularity and ineffectiveness. A Review of the role of the Commissions should be undertaken to sharpen up their liaison and their focus on providing effective remedies rather than just going through formal procedures. People must have effective remedies to injustice – but at the same time there must be a reasonably speedy end to complaint processes.

The principal weapon to challenge arbitrary government action is judicial review. In Scotland we have fewer of these than in England and 76% of them are to do with immigration issues. Many other challenges arise from cases brought within the criminal law area. Whilst these are vital, why are we not getting more cases on housing, welfare rights, education or planning? One reason, related to the size of the jurisdiction, may be the lack of sufficient legal expertise and the fact that such cases in small numbers are uneconomic to take. In Scotland, the role of bodies like Castlemilk or Govan Law Centres has been a pioneering one but Law Centres are not as common as in England. An expansion in this area would add considerably to public access to justice but perhaps there are issues too both of legal training and the ethos of the legal profession in Scotland.

Human rights analysis is not the speciality of MPs/MSPs and fundamental change often requires an external challenge such as an adverse inspection report, unflattering litigation or heavy media publicity to act as a driver for change. Following an adverse inspection report at Carstairs State Hospital, Professor Alan Miller, now Chair of the Scottish Human Rights Commission, was asked to carry out a human rights review of the State Hospital which wrought significant changes in practice.

The ECHR also has identified that there are major benefits to be obtained from inspection agencies and regulatory bodies adopting an explicit human rights approach – something I raised myself some time ago with the Auditor General for Scotland without much success.

Global Human Rights

Let me turn to human rights at a more international or global level. There are various levers that can be brought to bear here – legal rights against governments and corporations certainly, but also the use of the power of governments, the role of international bodies, the financial resource that can be deployed and the ethos and practice of large companies. None of us who have witnessed the collapse of the international banking structures as a result in essence of the abandonment of traditional prudence and ethics by, not least, the Scottish banks, can have any doubt about how crucial this all is to the rights and the quality of life of people across the globe.

Let us consider some of the challenges identified by the Institute for Human Rights and Business (which the UK government helps to fund).

There are of course obvious issues of tacking discrimination (for example, women's rights, LGBT rights and respect for minority religious rights), but there are also major labour market and resource issues – not just of fair trade and resource exploitation, but of human trafficking, child labour and forced labour, of the living wage and youth employment, of due diligence in sourcing goods relative to employment.

Behind these issues lie literally millions of tales of personal horror, deprivation, exploitation, corruption, sexual abuse, slavery and resource disasters – like the lives and deaths of the more than 1,000 workers earning an average of

$38 a month who died in the Rana Plaza factory collapse in Bangladesh in 2013.

These issues can be highly complex for companies operating in poorer parts of the world or in areas ravaged by civil war, terrorism, or foreign intervention. Countries like this badly need economic activity, employment for their young people and greater civil security, but economic activity has to be sustainable, and must foster and enforce corporate cultures which respect human rights. There must be universal criteria for operating in conflict zones, clear human rights responsibilities of corporate water users and water and sanitation service providers. Not least there are issues of tax justice and revenue transparency.

This whole area is shot through with hugely difficult dilemmas for government, as the example of China makes clear. China will soon be the largest economy in the world, the Chinese have considerable financial clout and investment potential but unfortunately they are not so good at protecting human rights. The balancing act between developing good relations and growing business with China whilst trying to jog them along on human rights is difficult. Alex Salmond got this wrong by snubbing the Dalai Lama on his visit to Scotland in 2012, apparently at the behest of the Chinese, even although both the Prime Minister and the Deputy Prime Minister had met him in London the previous month. It appears that Chinese trade and a couple of giant pandas were more important to the First Minister than human rights abuses by the Chinese in Tibet.

These are huge, global issues which require the clout of significant governments to tackle them. There have been important initiatives such as the Kimberley Process to eliminate trade in conflict diamonds or the Dhaka Principles for Migration with Dignity. The Gangmasters' Licensing Authority in the UK is widely regarded as one of the most successful models globally for regulating low-wage labour providers. Their remit currently covers agriculture, forestry, horticulture, shellfish gathering, food and drink processing and packaging. I understand that this success was not achieved without a lot of collaborative work between the Government and various NGOs including the IHRB and Oxfam.

In June 2011, the UN Human Rights Council endorsed the *UN Guiding Principles for Business and Human Rights* - the first corporate human rights responsibility initiative to be endorsed by the UN – stimulated in part by a meeting hosted by the SHRC in Edinburgh in 2010. The Ruggie Principles insist on the State's duty to protect against human rights abuses by business enterprises, through regulation, policymaking, investigation, and enforcement – while businesses must act with due diligence to avoid infringing on the rights of others, to address negative impacts – and to remedy infringements. In September 2013, the United Kingdom became the first country to set out an Action Plan on Business and Human Rights, providing a guidance framework to companies on integrating human rights into their activities.

The United Kingdom exercises very considerable soft power through its embassies and missions abroad – there are around 50 in Africa alone – through the significance of the City of London as a global centre, and through the UK's importance within the G7, the EU, the Commonwealth, the United Nations and a host of other international bodies. That is not to say the UK always gets its way or always gets it right, but it is noteworthy that we are the second highest aid donor in the world, one of the few to reach the UN 0.7% of GDP target, where the quality and impact of the aid is widely acknowledged.

Liberal Democrats should insist that the United Kingdom sets the standard in ensuring that business conforms to high and sustainable human rights standards.

The level of abuse and exploitation across the world by national and trans-national corporations is a major factor in the problems, particularly of the Third World and of areas of conflict. Is it time for a major initiative, equivalent to that which established the European Convention itself, to establish an International Human Rights Business and Employment Charter and to back it up with strengthened judicial machinery to enforce it?

But, in any event, a human rights framework, championed at senior levels, acts as the internal challenge function in an organisation, ensuring that human rights are integrated into key areas of policy and practice – like a magnet pulling services in the direction that best supports the dignity, respect, equality and autonomy of those that use them. Leadership, by politicians, by Chief Executives, Board members and senior staff of public bodies is vital in establishing an active and embracing human rights culture and showing how it fits in with other corporate agendas.

The arms trade merits a book by itself. In 2007, legal arms sales around the world were estimated at around $60 billion[58] – dominated by the five permanent members of the UN Security Council. Some of this is legitimate support for and trade with friendly democratic governments – but some of the largest purchasers are in the Middle East and South and East Asia. In 2010, the UK Government's Human Rights Annual Report identified 26 "countries of concern" – but approved arms export licences to 16 of them, including Syria, Somalia, Libya and Pakistan.

I have not the expertise to draw conclusions on this: suffice to say there are serious issues raised as to how far the "legal" arms trade contributes to the undermining of human rights in at least some of these countries.

---

[58] Rachel Stohl and Suzette Grillot – *The International Arms Trade* – Polity Press 2009, p 187 (quoted by Campaign Against Arms Trade)

I want to see a world where the power of governments, of courts, of bureaucracies, of public opinion is operated at the right level to stop abuses of human rights effectively and pro-actively, and where institutions, private and public, act to high standards that enhance rather than damage freedom and life chances. There is a huge task ahead in improving and delivering human rights – to secure the formal commitment of government to international agreements, to change the culture of public bodies in Scotland, to get international companies linked to this country committed to and delivering human rights practices in the complex and challenging activities they undergo particularly abroad, to recognise that the human rights of a garment worker in Bangladesh, a coffee farmer in Africa, or a child transported across the globe for sexual exploitation or labour are human rights for which we have responsibility.

Agenda for Human Rights

There is a substantial and congenial agenda for Liberal Democrats in the field of human rights at home and abroad. The process of establishing a written constitution for a federal Britain could be the driver of change, putting at centre stage the question of what sort of country we want to be, what are our aspirations and our core values.

The Scottish Parliament should undoubtedly establish a Human Rights Committee whilst a successor Scottish government to the SNP should review key legislation as part of post legislative scrutiny to ensure that it fully protects civil rights in Scotland.

The Campbell Commission[59] spoke of a duty on all levels of government to work for the elimination of poverty and of Beveridge's other "giants" – squalor, ignorance, want, idleness and disease. Economic and social rights like these

---

[59] Campbell Commission c2 para 86

are recognised by international human rights instruments[60] and governments are obliged to respect and protect them and to take "progressive action" towards their fulfillment, but they inevitably provide more challenges both in defining minimum standards and in enforcement than traditional civil liberties.

Most human rights campaigners would insist that the United Kingdom should act further on the remaining Human Rights accords[61] to which we are not fully committed or where we don't allow individual complaint – and identify what it needs to do to sign up fully and ensure substantial compliance. This might very well be a good thing but my personal view is that a strengthened emphasis in Parliament on effective governmental action to secure economic and social rights is more important.

In the area of personal information, the UK government has committed to the establishment of a Privacy and Civil Liberties Oversight Board – but the scope for it to be instead a Ministry of Truth in the Orwellian sense is impressively high. This area needs international principles and norms derived from the ECHR and effective international enforcement. We need a "Digital Bill of Rights" to establish norms of acceptable behaviour by governments, individuals and companies in the sphere of the internet and social media. This in turn requires expert analysis and advice on the issues.

For the global operation of large corporations, we need a major drive to establish, enforce and provide judicial machinery to control the illegal and exploitative activities of

---

[60] Universal Declaration on Human Rights (UN – 1948);
International Covenant on Economic, Social and Cultural Rights (UN - 1966)
[61] UN Convention on the Rights of the Child has been ratified by the UK – some people would like to see it incorporated into UK law as such. The Optional Protocol to the ICoESC Rights (2008) has been acceded to for example by Belgium, Finland and Portugal but not UK

companies – perhaps as a first step a modernised International Labour Organisation to ensure higher standards on all matters affecting employment and the workforce on an international level.

The UN Guiding Principles for Business and Human Rights are a small start but this needs to develop into an enforceable Charter of Human Rights in Business which is empowered to follow through abuses to their source and deal with them, both domestically and through international bodies.

But, above all, the cause of human rights needs "the spirit of liberty" – an active commitment to civic and political liberty in our Parliaments, our institutions and our society. The spirit of liberty can deliver practical remedies in practical cases, and be effective regardless of constitutions – but it requires an independent judiciary, not elected, not subject to pressure from the Sun or the Record, and able to hold to account the excesses of power of governments and parliaments – and global giants – who go beyond their entitlements.

The prize of a strengthened commitment to human rights is a world where human life, freedom and individual wellbeing and opportunity are respected and protected. Few things could be more worthwhile.

Strategy, Power and Values

From coalitions with the Conservatives to a coalition with the Conservatives

Ross Finnie

Introduction

In the 19th and 20th centuries there were three peace-time coalitions involving the Liberal Party, either in whole or in part, each of which was a coalitions with the Conservative Party. In the early part of the 21st century, the Liberal Democrats formed a coalition with the Conservatives at a UK level but the political positioning of the Liberals and then the Liberal Democrats, throughout the post-war period, would not have anticipated such a development. This short chapter looks at some aspects of the early coalitions that provide some interesting perspectives, narrates a lengthy period of trying to realign the "Left" of British politics and considers the most recent experiences of coalitions noting a distinct rightward shift in political positioning.

The early coalitions

The 1895–1905 coalition was between the Conservatives and the Liberal Unionists. The Liberal Unionists had formed in 1886 following the split in the Liberal Party over home rule for Ireland and the Unionists had a long-term alliance with the Conservatives until agreement was reached for a coalition to fight the 1895 General Election. The Liberal

Unionists found maintaining a separate identity difficult in coalition and outwith the coalition faced pressure from a resurgent Liberal Party. Between 1903 and 1906, eight Liberal Unionist free trade MPs rejoined the Liberals. In 1905 Balfour resigned as Prime Minister being replaced by Henry Campbell- Bannerman who went on to win a landslide victory for the Liberals in 1906. The Liberal Unionists never recovered from their time in coalition and eventually, in 1912, merged entirely into the Conservative Party.

The 1916–1922 Lloyd George Coalition between the Conservatives and a substantial part of the Liberal Party was created with the bold ambition of building a "new world" after the war. Liberal participation in the coalition was coloured throughout by the manoeuvres, at the outset, that saw Asquith replaced by Lloyd George, mainly at the Conservatives' behest, and complaints by many in the Party at the total absence of transparency in the way in which the coalition was formed. The Liberal Ministers in the coalition were perceived as weak and their domestic and foreign policies were heavily criticised. In 1922 Conservative backbenchers rebelled and brought the coalition down. In the subsequent General Election Liberals who had been in government found themselves arguing rather tortuously that they had been effective in making a reactionary government less reactionary than it otherwise might have been. In the election both Liberal factions fared badly and were outpolled by the Labour Party.

The National Government of 1931–1940 was formed as a result of the collapse of the Labour minority administration in the face of economic crisis. Britain faced a budget deficit of £120 million in 1932-33 or 3.1% of GDP. This compares with an overall deficit of 7.5 per cent of GDP and a structural deficit of 5.3% of GDP faced by the Conservative/Liberal Democrat coalition of 2010. The fiscal consolidation undertaken by the National Government was therefore much smaller than that of the current coalition but was implemented more quickly. The burden of deficit reduction was effected fairly evenly between tax increases and spending cuts concentrated heavily on unemployment benefit and public sector pay. The Liberals supported the fiscal measures but remained split, as they had been for the previous decade, over the principle of defending free trade. The Liberal Party split three ways: the mainstream under Sir Herbert Samuel left the coalition in 1932 having failed to secure guarantees over free trade; followers of Sir John Simon pledged unconditional support; and Lloyd George's faction took little or no part in the coalition. Although the mainstream had resigned over a matter of principle, the Party was still associated with its part in the coalition and at the General Election of 1935 the Liberals were reduced to only 21 seats from the 59 won in 1929.

A fundamental difference between these coalitions and the current Westminster coalition on the one hand and the Scottish Liberal Democrat coalitions of 1999 and 2003 in the Scottish Parliament is that the three earlier coalitions were formed before the respective general elections. Current thinking is that: political parties should contest elections as independent entities; the electorate should decide the composition of the parliament; and the leaders of the political parties should respond to the decision of the electorate. Some Liberal historians argue the contrary position that by forming a pre-election agreement this gave them a legitimacy not enjoyed by the 1999, 2003 and 2010 coalitions. Interestingly, following the election results of 1895, 1918 and 1931 the Conservatives could have formed a majority government had not the pre-election agreements been in place.

The post-war period

The revival of the Party started in the mid 1950s after Jo Grimond was elected leader. Grimond was an immensely charismatic leader who wanted to recreate a radical Liberal Party having amongst its aims the capacity to challenge socialism with its platform of state-ownership. Indeed in 1958 Grimond first advocated what he called "a realignment of the left". His successor, Jeremy Thorpe, pursued a similar political line but his only offer of power came from the right in the shape of an offer of coalition from Prime Minister Edward Heath following the February 1974 General Election. Thorpe never thought it was a starter but did ask if there might be any prospect of electoral reform. All Thorpe was offered was the possibility of a Speakers Conference which did not help to overcome three fundamental problems: first, the increase in the Liberal vote had been largely against the Tories' inability to deal with the worsening economic and industrial situation; second, Heath had called the election and lost his majority; and third, the Tories and Liberals together still had no majority – the Ulster Unionists of Paisleyites and Powellites were unattractive bedfellows.

After a short interregnum, David Steel became leader in 1976 and, in his first Assembly speech in September that year, declared amongst other things: "We must be bold enough to deploy the coalition case positively." Just over six months later, Steel took the Liberals into the Lib-Lab Agreement (or Lib-Lab Pact as it became known) from March 1977 to June 1978. Today, it might more properly have been called a confidence and supply agreement. It was born out of the prevailing economic crisis and it tried to secure progress on Liberal touchstones such as devolution and electoral reform. Constitutional reform was not achieved but the Treasury, under Chancellor Denis Healey but with John Pardoe's Liberal influence, saw inflation fall from 20 per cent to 9 per cent and as a result mortgage interest rates fell from 12.5% to 8.5 per cent. Although Pardoe's influence was widely acknowledged, the Party itself was not seen as having sufficient influence. The Liberals got almost no credit for their part in helping to stabilise the economy and, as a result, the Pact proved to be electorally damaging.

In 1981 the "Gang of Four" broke away from the Labour Party to form the SDP. By March of that year the Alliance between the Liberals and the SDP had been formed to fight elections on a common policy platform. At the 1983 General Election the Alliance won 25.4 per cent of the popular vote but won only 23 seats. Four years later the vote fell back to 22.6 per cent and Steel proposed a merger which took place in March 1988. Paddy Ashdown became the first elected leader of the Liberal Democrats and after the 1992 General Election Ashdown delivered his "Chard Speech" in which he signalled his willingness to work with Labour to defeat the Conservatives. This thinking was developed further into what became known as Ashdown's "Project" to create a coalition of the left. The Party's Federal Conference of 1995 formally abandoned the position of "equidistance", taking up a position closer to Labour and in March 1996 the Liberal Democrats entered into formal collaboration with the Labour Party on constitutional reform under Bob McLennan and Robin Cook.

In May 1997 New Labour won a landslide victory but Ashdown still seemed intent on forming a coalition with New Labour. This led the Federal Conference of September 1998 to pass the so called "triple lock" amendment: no coalition agreement without (i) agreement of both a majority of the members of the Parliamentary Party of the House of Commons and the Federal Executive (ii) unless there is a three quarters majority of each of these groups in favour, the consent of the majority of those voting at a special conference is needed, and (iii) unless there is a two-thirds majority of those present and voting at the special

Conference in favour of the proposal, the consent of a majority of all members voting in a ballot. There was no coalition, therefore but Ashdown and Blair still went ahead with forming a Joint Cabinet Committee in July 1997 to work on largely constitutional matters. The joint Committee foundered on PR and ended in January 1999 – the "Project" was over. Nevertheless it had solidified a programme of constitutional reform which was largely implemented after 1997 – not least in terms of devolution and the incorporation of the European Convention on Human Rights into domestic law.

Recent coalitions

The Scotland Act 1998 and the Government of Wales Act 1998 not only established the Scottish Parliament and the National Assembly for Wales but also ensured that they would be elected by proportional representation. Jim Wallace, then Leader of the Scottish Liberal Democrats, made clear the Party would be fighting the 1999 Scottish Election to win the maximum number of seats possible and refused to be drawn on questions about possible coalitions. Wallace did, however get the agreement of the Party as to how any coalition was to be agreed. The 1999 election result produced a hung Parliament with Labour as the largest minority group. The ensuing coalition talks were made easier by the fact that in creating New Labour, Tony Blair had adopted a more social democrat policy stance which, whilst far from being Liberal Democrat, nevertheless was closer to the Liberal Democrat position than previously.

The coalition talks had their difficulties and the biggest stumbling block was over the Liberal Democrat commitment to abolish student fees. The incoming Labour Government at Westminster had accepted the Deering Report and introduced student fees with the three Labour

Ministers[62] who were part of the negotiating team for the Scottish Parliament all voting in favour. The Cubie Committee, established, as a deal breaker, to examine student finance in further and higher education, proposed the abolition of student fees with a graduate contribution towards funding poorer students. The proposal wasn't easy to sell; it didn't compromise the Scottish Party's ability to continue to campaign for the abolition of the graduate contribution but it was a salutary lesson on the need to think through how to protect key policy commitments on matters of principle in coalition negotiations.

The first Coalition Agreement was for the fixed period of the Parliament 1999 – 2003. The reality of collective responsibility – Liberal Democrat members had to vote for all policies in the Agreement not just the Liberal Democrat bits – was the first of many lessons to be learnt in coalition. Another was the need to establish a press office that could positively and effectively sell the Liberal Democrat line. The Scottish Liberal Democrats badly underestimated the importance of a strong press office and, facing openly hostile criticism by sections of the tabloid press, suffered badly in the early months. The coalition went its full term but, towards the end, it was mainly Ministers who spoke for the coalition whilst the rest of the Party got on with fighting the election as an independent Party. The Scottish election of 2003 produced broadly similar Parliamentary arithmetic as in 1999 with the Party again winning 17 seats. A second coalition agreement was negotiated with the Labour Party for the second term of the Parliament from 2003 – 2007. After eight years in government Scottish Liberal Democrats could point to upwards of 75% of its manifesto commitments having been delivered including: abolition of tuition fees, freedom of information legislation; land reform; setting

---

[62] Donald Dewar, Henry McLeish and Sam Galbraith

targets for renewable energy; free personal care for the elderly; and PR for local government elections.

The Welsh Assembly elections of 1999 also produced a hung Assembly but Labour ran a minority government until 2001 when they entered into a coalition agreement with the Welsh Liberal Democrats under Mike German. The Welsh Liberal Democrats also succeeded in getting key policies implemented including: smaller class sizes; free school milk; and a freeze on prescription charges. Unfortunately, improving the overall performance of the Welsh Assembly Government only helped the Labour Party to win an overall majority in the 2003 elections.

The 2010 Westminster General Election resulted in a hung Parliament against the background of the worst economic crisis in living memory. The Labour Prime Minister, Gordon Brown, bearing a heavy culpability for the crisis, was keen for Labour to cling on to office, his party less so. The Liberal Democrats had indicated a willingness to negotiate with the largest party and talks began with the Conservatives. Apparently, the Liberal Democrat negotiators originally supported a confidence and supply agreement but were persuaded into a coalition on the grounds that majority governments took harder decisions. That would certainly have been a lesson to have been drawn from the Lib-Lab Pact of 1977 but, given that the economic situation and banking crisis were the driving imperatives, it doesn't wholly explain why the negotiating team entered into a full blown coalition agreement that envisaged policy development across all aspects of government. Perhaps the reason is to be found in the combination of the rightward shift in the Liberal Democrat position under Nick Clegg's leadership and a major move to the centre by the Conservative Party as David Cameron tried to position his party as "liberal conservatives" that had brought the two Parties much closer in policy terms.

There appear to have been faults in the construction of the administrative arrangements for the Coalition. The Scottish experience was that the First Minister and the majority party had a considerable ability, by virtue of their control of key parts of the government machine, to set the tone and mood music of the administration. However they were not in a position to make unilateral announcements on behalf of the government without full clearance across government. This meant that Scottish Liberal Democrat Ministers were largely able to block unpalatable proposals and secure policy arrangements the Party was more comfortable with before either side lost face.

The 2010 Westminster coalition by contrast appears to have been punctuated by Prime Ministerial and Ministerial announcements which gave the appearance of not being known about or signed up to in advance. Notable examples include the NHS reforms, David Cameron's exercise of the UK veto at the EU, the notorious "immigrants go home" poster campaign launched by the Home Office and repeated controversies over terrorism and privacy legislation. It is difficult to conceive how any of these things could have emerged from a government with Liberal Democrat support. The whole concept of collective cabinet responsibility has been heavily eroded.

The Liberal Democrats deserve credit for some signal achievements by the coalition: raising the income tax threshold: securing a referendum on AV (although holding the referendum on the date of the Scottish Elections created a perception that the Liberal Democrats were more interested in constitutional change than sorting the economy); implementing the pupil premium in England; carrying through major reforms of pensions and re-establishing the link with earnings; and setting up the green investment bank. The change of political direction under Clegg, however, means that these achievements have to be set against other, less palatable things done by the Party:

supporting a greater degree of privatisation in the NHS; abandoning the abolition of tuition fees (in England); and supporting elements of welfare reform that have been described by the Poverty Truth Commission in Scotland as: "deepening inequality...[the changes] being felt disproportionately, by the very poorest and most vulnerable in our society." The overwhelming majority of the Party, nevertheless, have been prepared to sustain Clegg in office despite concerns about his distinctly economic liberal stance. Indeed, Paddy Ashdown, author of the "Project" will hear no criticism of Clegg or his political stance. The irony is that had Ashdown supported such a political stance he would never have been elected as leader of the Party.

Conclusion

Coalitions and agreements with other parties have not been an unqualified success and this has resulted in frequent calls, from within the Party, never to enter into such arrangements. Despite these calls it is difficult, if not impossible, to disagree with the general principles enunciated by Grimond, Johnston and Steel, in 1974, that a serious political Party and especially one that espoused proportional representation should always be prepared at least to consider a coalition. As ever the devil is in the detail. The early coalitions suffered from the absence of a written agreement but much more so from splits within the Party some of which were exacerbated by the formation of the coalition. With the exception of the Scottish coalitions, the Party's experience of coalitions and pacts has been electorally damaging.

This latter point can be traced largely to a failure, either to define the principal purpose of the coalition and not allow that purpose to be diffused, or to prosecute and relentlessly promote that principal purpose and the Party's role in it. The coalition of 2010 is a case in point. The imperative of tackling the economic crisis was undisputed. The Labour

Party had lost credibility over its handling of the economy and therefore a coalition with the Conservatives, much of whose manifesto the Party had opposed, seemed the more plausible alternative. Indeed, Steel's initial description of the coalition - as a "business arrangement born of necessity to clear up the country's dire financial debt and that it should never be portrayed as anything else" - was not borne out by the coalition agreement or by the breadth of policies prosecuted by the coalition. It can still be argued that the Party underestimates the negotiating power of the party providing a government with its majority and, given that a very high percentage of any government's workload is administrative rather than political, it is not necessary for a coalition agreement to provide for policy development and legislation across every sphere of government.

Finally, there is the image and mood music of the government. These were set in the early days, with the appearance of Clegg and Cameron in the "rose garden" and their camaraderie on the front-benches which created the perception of political closeness. This was followed by the loss of trust caused by the tuition fees debacle – on an issue so central to our campaign and image and our core support. Arguably the electoral disasters which have befallen the Liberal Democrats since then have their roots in these early mistakes. Whether the exercise of taking a Party which had spent 60 years establishing itself as a radical party of the centre-left into a coalition with the Conservatives could ever have been achieved without electoral damage remains a moot point. But it is highly relevant to speculate on whether things would have been different – if damage limitation would have been more effective - if the Liberal Democrats had negotiated a narrower Coalition agreement and focused on sorting out the financial and economic crisis. On any view, Coalition government comes with a major health warning for the minority party.

The Liberalism of Jo Grimond and the Politics of the Coalition

Willis Pickard

Notoriously, neither the Conservative nor Labour Party knew what to do when the 2010 general election failed to give either of them an overall majority. Despite the opinion polls during the election campaign neither was prepared for coalition. The London-based media were unprepared, too. Failing to look north to the Scottish experience, some even denounced the possibility of coalition as unBritish.

The Liberal Democrats on the other hand (like the predecessor Liberal Party) were flexible of mind and prepared for most eventualities, including the need for the party in the country to debate and decide on terms for coalition. So, whatever the rights and wrongs of the agreement reached between the Conservatives and Liberal Democrats, no one can say that the latter blundered into the unforeseen. (Conservative backbenchers and activists might have a more reasonable grouse about their party's behaviour.)

The 1945 and 1950 general elections were the last in which Liberals had professed ambition, however unrealistic, to form a government. Since then they have become practised in seeking ways of exerting influence on and/or sharing power. They are also better historians than most Tories or Labour supporters, for whom two-party politics and a decisive election result are assumed to be the norm. Liberals know that only since the Second World War could politics be seen in terms of a straight Right-Left choice. Away back in the Liberal heyday Gladstone enjoyed no dependable overall majority in the Commons. Forced reliance on Irish Nationalists led him to a Home Rule Bill that split his party. Campbell-Bannerman and Asquith from 1906–10 did have a Commons majority, but thereafter the Irish had again to be accommodated. As for Lloyd George he, as always, turned circumstances to his advantage when he carried wartime coalition into the 1918 election and left his own party divided and stranded. His ambitious and forward-looking programme for the 1929 election would have needed coalition to implement since there was no prospect of an outright Liberal mandate.

The next quarter of a century saw a struggle for the very survival of the Liberal Party. In the contest between capital and labour there seemed no role for a third force. When Jo Grimond became leader in 1956 his tiny band of MPs had little clout, but his enthusiasm for new ideas began to bring academics and students to the fold. The question was how to turn renewed influence into votes and seats. In 1955 only Grimond himself had won his seat against both Conservative and Labour opposition. The need was to regain intellectual credibility for a party beholden to neither of the larger forces. So Grimond went for the big issues – tackling industrial relations, embracing membership of the Common Market, promoting a radical alternative. Fortunately, the 1959 election, while disappointing in producing no Liberal breakthrough, gave the Conservatives a comfortable majority and removed for the time being the endless question of which major party the Liberals would support in the event of a hung parliament.

It is important to remember that for a man of Grimond's generation the idea of coalition was more threatening than inviting. He had come to adulthood while the Liberals were divided and lost in coalitions. As a candidate and MP in the late forties and fifties he endured the tensions between colleagues who favoured siding with one or other of the big parties. Churchill as Prime Minister from 1951 brushed down his old Liberal clothes in an attempt to forge an anti-Soclalist alliance. Signs of Liberal revival, tentative before 1959 and much clearer in the early 1960s, were mainly evident in Conservative areas, while Grimond's thinking and that of his bright recruits led towards a "realignment of the left", detaching modernising and moderate Labour supporters from diehard Socialists and deadwood trade-union nominees. The dilemma was insoluble unless the number of Liberal MPs rose dramatically or the Labour Party split. (As late as 1970 and 1974, I along with all other Liberal candidates was instructed never on any account to state a public preference for Tory or Labour as a coalition partner.) The prospect of electoral reform or "fairer votes" was always held out by the party as the way to break the bi-party duopoly, but only sufficient political clout could enforce change and that presupposed success under the existing voting system.

When in 1964 Labour came to power with a majority of only four, Grimond made no attempt to offer Wilson parliamentary stability, and the prospect of exerting influence diminished when the 1966 general election gave Labour a comfortable majority without significantly altering the number of Liberal MPs. Grimond retired as leader; but his appetite for new ideas and challenging orthodoxy (including within his party) increased. He came out in favour of an electoral pact with the Scottish National Party to the dismay of many Scottish Liberals, who saw inconsistency with his refusal to side with any opposing party south of the border. In February 1974 he joined his parliamentary colleagues, however, in turning aside Heath's offer of various levels of cooperation, even coalition, as a way of maintaining a Conservative Government. Electoral reform remained off the agenda, the Tories had lost an election they had called, and so the Liberals would remain in opposition.

Coalition or at least cooperation with a Labour Government ought to have been a more congenial prospect to Grimond and Liberal activists. But when an embattled Callaghan held out the prospect of Liberal MPs being consulted on government policies, Grimond upset the new Liberal leader, David Steel, by voicing his objections. With hindsight we can see why. Liberals would incur opposition for supporting an administration made unpopular for mishandling the economy, but would not be able to impress their own policies on the Government. Interestingly, the Lib-Lab pact was dissolved a year before the 1979 election. The Liberals had time to regain a measure of electoral appeal. Steel was vindicated but Grimond had been right to decry an arrangement which addressed only numbers in the voting lobby at Westminster. Liberals had no mechanism for promoting their own policies. Another opportunity for asserting Liberal relevance went by the board.

The arrival of the Social Democratic Party offered a new opportunity and one that exactly reflected the long-held aspirations of Grimond. Although the groundwork for an alliance between the new party and the Liberals was prepared by Steel and Roy Jenkins, they must have appreciated that what they were planning was what Grimond had begun talking about in the late 1950s. Inevitably and debilitatingly, attention turned to the division of constituencies between the two parties. But Grimond insisted that the big picture was important. Get the major policies right and their appeal to the electorate might carry the day. The appeal was well judged. Failure in its execution was down to the difficulties of running two parties in harmony, the public's puzzlement about who was boss (Steel or Jenkins; Steel or Owen?) and the deep roots of the two big parties, which were shaken but not fatally disturbed. The public professed admiration for what the Gang of Four and the Alliance promised but the novelty wore off – rather like the short-lived surge of support for the LibDems in the 2010 election.

Grimond underestimated the forces of conservatism that were reinforced by the unhappy coincidence of the Falklands war which turned attention from domestic politics to the South Atlantic. The former leader, however, threw his weight behind the electoral pact that was needed if his party and the SDP were to maximise the third-force effect. He urged the Liberal Assembly:

"I beg of you to seize this chance – do not get bogged down in the niceties of innumerable policies. I spent my life fighting against too much policy in the Liberal Party! I do not believe that we have to have a policy on dog licences and the details of world government. But also make quite sure that your major policies are right and that you are going to defend them – because you may have to put them into practice." [63]

That final admonition about defending only the defensible may strike a chord with those LibDem MPs who in later coalition have been faced with reneging on a pledge to students.

Grimond did not live to see his party take a role in government with all the attendant stresses, strains and electoral scepticism. He did not even see the attempt by Steel's successor, Paddy Ashdown, to work with a Labour Government in the interests of constitutional reform. Tony Blair in his pomp did not need the Liberal Democrats. Grimond always emphasised that a realignment of the left involved electoral reform. In the late 1990s that was not in

---

[63] Michael McManus *Jo Grimond: Towards the Sound of Gunfire*. Edinburgh 2001 p.350

the interests of the Labour Party. Liberal Democrats were left on their own to build in Parliament and local government and to summon up the forces of protest when Blair's Government was lured into the mire of Iraq. The problem for today's Liberal Democrats is that electoral reforms are again off the agenda (because this time it is not in the interest of the Conservative Party). But as a party of government the Liberal Democrats are exposed to unpopularity. One of the criteria which Grimond regarded as essential in creating a strong third force was electoral reform. One can argue that the setback of the AV referendum in 2011 is just another example of the reluctance of the British state to modernise its constitution. Neither the first nor the second Reform Act in the 19th century was carried at the first attempt. Try, try and try again is an admirable political injunction. For the LibDems the question is how long we must keep trying and whether the existing system will exact unjustified punishment while we wait.

Would Grimond have approved of LibDem participation in the present coalition? That is the kind of question a historian should avoid - *autres temps, autres moeurs*. David Steel, however, was willing to chance his arm in the course of a lecture in Orkney last year to mark the centenary of Grimond's birth.[64] "Decidedly yes," was his answer. He gave as a reason Grimond's reluctance in 1974 to rule out a coalition with the Conservatives in any circumstances, not least because that would be inconsistent with support for proportional representation. Steel went on to say that Grimond would not have approved of all that the coalition had done, instancing the student fees debacle. He would have been dubious about the AV referendum and the "laundry list" of supposed LibDem achievements in

---

[64] David Steel *Jo Grimond 1913–2013* in Journal of Liberal History (Issue 80, Autumn 2013) p.13

government. As Grimond had said in 1964, the important thing was facing up to the economic situation. Steel then listed Liberal principles and values that Grimond had embodied and were still relevant today. They included support for democracy in industry and a land tax.

Coalition is for the tough minded. That was Grimond's own verdict. In his *Memoirs*[65] he wrote: "Nowadays the cry for a coalition often degenerates into the plaintive whine of those too supine to steel themselves for the sort of decisions which need to be taken." He went on to distinguish, as he had throughout his political life, between those who believe in the benefits of an ever-growing state and those who believe that values lie in the individual and are threatened by collectivism. We may respect our opponents but should not pretend that we are all political brothers under the skin. It is hard to imagine him admiring the Cameron/Clegg love-in of Rose Garden days. On the other hand, the coalition as it has developed has imposed mental toughness on ministers previously unexposed to hard choices. Grimond as a product of the privileged classes never expected to find political brotherhood among Conservatives, for he knew them too well. He would have been perturbed by the weakness of the last Labour Government, spending money that did not exist and as a result condemning to years of austerity the poor whom Labour supposedly exists to protect.

Brown's Government, well stuffed with Scots, should have been better prepared for minority government or coalition when it failed to achieve a majority in 2010. The party had successfully shared power with the Liberal Democrats in the first two administrations of the Scottish Parliament. The electoral system was designed to make shared power the norm. Hardened Labour politicians who regarded Liberal Democrats as naive dilettantes were surprised that the party's ministers led by Jim Wallace and

---

[65] Jo Grimond *Memoirs* London 1979 p.262

Ross Finnie were tough and thorough. It is true that after two terms neither of the coalition partners quite knew what it wanted to do in a third term. Four years later the electorate showed that it could outwit the constitution makers by giving the SNP an overall majority, which was supposed to be all but impossible. Hard though the result was for Labour and the Liberal Democrats , it was in its cackhanded way a vindication of democracy.

So we have had a British coalition born of a constitution designed to make it highly unlikely; and in Scotland a single-party Government where coalition was designed to be the norm. Jo Grimond, who had a keen eye for the quirkiness of politics, would surely be amused.

Will we, either in Britain or in Scotland, come to the European view that coalitions are to be expected and, more important, are comprehensible to the voters? For an answer, let's bypass Belgium with its linguistic politics and ability to get along without any government at all for months on end. Rather, revisit *Borgen,* the television series that not only made Danish politics interesting but showed, better than any constitutional textbook, how coalition government works. The point was that coalitions were built – and sometimes fell apart – on the basis that voters knew what the parties stood for. So a coalition with a strong conservative component would aim to reduce public spending, whereas a phalanx of Green ministers would be against nuclear power and keen on birds. Never underestimate voter sophistication. The Irish, with skills honed at the Curragh, calculate how to place their complicated preference votes to ensure that the widow of the late lamented TD inherits his seat. The Germans, grateful for the fair federalism imposed by the occupying British, know how to maintain stability, which traditionally included keeping the Free Democrats as part of every coalition; unfortunately for European liberalism, the voters finally pulled the rug from under them.

There is a lesson from the sad exit of the Free Democrats from the Bundestag. They lost their distinctive message. They appeared creatures of government for government's sake. For Liberal Democrats here, there is an uncomfortable message. Don't believe because you have marked up successes as part of a coalition that renewed participation is either a birthright or maybe even desirable. Of course a good record in government is important and must be made known to voters. Credibility after all is important, and for decades lack of experience in government was an electoral handicap to Liberals.

But as Grimond repeatedly emphasised, "for me the content of politics is all important." So leaving aside the merits and demerits of being in coalition at all, what would he have made of LibDem contribution to the coalition formed in 2010? He would surely have looked to evidence that the Government was acting on the Liberal principle of making life better for the individual, especially the individual whose lot had been hard. Having, late in his career, proposed student loans and education vouchers, he would surely have been distressed by the muddle, however well intentioned, that LibDem MPs got into over tuition fees. But that policy disaster should be set against successful policies implementing Liberal principle.

Reducing the tax burden on the less well off would be one. Steve Webb's changes to pension regulations are another – classically liberal in origin. Grimond, like Gladstone, wanted to remove barriers to individual choice. So it is right for the recipient of an accumulated pension to decide what to do with it. However, recent so-called radicalism in another Westminster department, Education, would not have met Grimond's favour. Michael Gove sought to bring back academic rigour and national pride to the English school curriculum. Grimond was the product of a privileged, traditional education at Eton and Oxford. Throughout his life, he was stimulated by academic debate.

But he professed to enjoy most the company of young students, and was rector of two Scottish universities. The self-confidence of today's students and their desire to explore new technologies and ways of learning and communicating would surely have reinforced Grimond's optimism about the young. Gove on the other hand wanted teachers to look back to an idealised society of grammar schools.

Grimond fought his early battles as party leader against Tories bemoaning the loss of empire. Yearning for the past remains a Conservative sentiment, pessimistic and debilitating. It leads to disillusionment with the political process, which Grimond fought to counter by reform of the institutions and mechanics of government. He would have regretted the failure of the coalition's attempts at electoral reform, half-hearted though they were. He would have predicted the rise of anti-politics – Farage today, Enoch Powell in the sixties. And he would have wondered why coalition ministers mired themselves in side-issues of welfare reform, like the "bedroom tax", while leaving untouched the abuses of tax-dodging big business and amoral international finance.

In the parlance of today's LibDem discourse we inevitably ask, was Grimond a "social Liberal" or an "economic Liberal"? It is not a helpful distinction, and I think it owes much to the notion that a large, grown-up party should demonstrate that it embraces different wings, even mutually suspicious factions. Grimond distrusted an overbearing state but wanted to use the power of government to make life better for his fellow citizens. The emphases in his thinking varied at different stages of his life. It is fair to suggest, as McManus does, that he moved in later years towards the classical hands-off liberalism of Gladstone and away from the interventionism of, say, Lloyd George. Policy debate of the kind Grimond stimulated does not produce consistency, for circumstances change and so does a lively mind. He did not always agree with himself and

155

certainly not with the self-righteousness of parties, even his own. When seeking re-election in Orkney and Shetland, he is claimed to have stopped at the ports all literature emanating from Liberal headquarters.

Bibliography

Jo Grimond wrote his own *Memoirs*. London 1979.

There are two recent biographies:

McManus Michael: *Jo Grimond: Towards the Sound of Gunfire*. Edinburgh 2001

Barberis Peter: *Liberal Lion: Jo Grimond, a Political Life*. London 2005

See also Steel David: *Jo Grimond 1913– 2013* in Journal of Liberal History (Issue 80, Autumn 2013) pp.8-14

The Coalition 2010– 2015 Lessons for Liberal Democrats

Caron Lindsay

I write this in the shadow of a roller coaster in Scotland's biggest theme park. It seems appropriate given the stomach-lurching nature of the last four years of Coalition Government with the Conservatives. There have been some highs as we've seen long-standing Liberal Democrat policies implemented, but there have also been significant electoral and personal consequences for the party as a whole.

It's all very different from the eight years when the Scottish Liberal Democrats were governing with Labour. Then, the two parties were able to enact truly radical legislation from free personal care to fair votes for local government to far more robust freedom of information legislation to the first smoking ban in the UK. It was a much easier time to be in charge. There was plenty money around. There were dangers, though. The swell of optimism which surrounded the creation of the Scottish Parliament could have led to disillusion and disappointment had it failed to deliver inspiring, meaningful and radical change. Crucially, the parties were not only much more compatible but the key players knew each other well. The years of joint working and negotiation on the Scottish Constitutional Convention had helped to form a mutual respect.

Compare and contrast with the rather more hostile environment which the UK faced just after the 2010 election. In the wake of the worst financial crisis and deepest recession in 80 years, the ink was barely dry on the note left by Labour's Chief Secretary to the Treasury, informing his successor that there was "no money left." The Liberal Democrats could only achieve a parliamentary majority with the Conservatives, a party with which they had little in common. In essence, the parties are fundamental opposites. While Conservatives want to keep things the same to serve established vested interests, Liberal Democrats want to shake things up, to take us further along the road to being the fair, free and open society that the vision in our constitution demands.

Three things have contributed more than any other to the party's current poor poll showings. A top-down reorganisation in the NHS, specifically ruled out in the Coalition Agreement, was enacted; welfare reforms, particularly the hated 'Bedroom Tax', proved controversial. Finally, and fundamentally, the breaking of a pledge to vote against any increase in tuition fees has torpedoed trust and credibility. So, we emerge to face the UK electorate in 2015 and the Scottish electorate in 2016 with the footprint of the electorate on our posterior. Having lost 2/3 of our MSPs in 2011, half our councillors in 2012 and our MEP in 2014, what lessons can the Scottish Liberal Democrats take from the experience and what principles should guide us? I set out 8 areas which, if the party gets right, could improve its fortunes should it find itself in government again.

1. Be honest about what we've done in UK coalition

Four years on, three of the four main priorities on the front of our 2010 manifesto have been implemented. Extra money is being given to support disadvantaged kids in school thanks to the Pupil Premium. The tax threshold has been raised for low and middle income earners, which has put more money back in their pockets. The first Green Investment Bank in the world has been established and there has been unprecedented investment in renewable energy. The fourth priority has been more difficult, however. House of Lords reform was blocked by a collusion of reactionary forces in Conservative and Labour parties. A referendum on changes to the voting system which, arguably, should never have made its way into the Coalition Agreement was lost and no progress made on party funding and the recall of MPs.

Our problem is that voters do not credit us with any of these things, nor of being responsible for the economic recovery. Perhaps a more candid approach to the realities of coalition government from the outset might have earned more respect from voters and made them more willing to listen when we talk about our achievements.

The realities of coalition government, though, make it impossible to deliver everything that we want. We should be clear about that and emphasise what we would do if we were in power on our own. Any voter who has ever been in a relationship or had to deal with any other human beings on anything will understand that you can't get your own way all of the time. We need to acknowledge that and then emphasise, in a constructive way, what we would do differently.

There is a great deal that we can be proud of. Much of our best work applies only in England but what we should do is to articulate the values on which we have based our decisions. There are some recurring themes which have underpinned our work: decentralisation (e.g. the City Deals and the Scotland Act), giving power back to the individual (shared parental leave, or giving people the right to marry the person they love), breaking down barriers (the global crusade against violence against women and girls or giving extra money to disadvantaged kids in school or improving mental health care and services) and protecting people from the abuse of power (e.g. a liberal solution on zero hours contracts, curbs on payday lenders, preventing the wholesale and illiberal retention of communications data).

This sort of theme-based thinking should replace our traditional way of writing a manifesto: picking a Government department and putting a list of policies underneath it. Of course we need to showcase our policies but they should be there as evidence of the values they represent.

2. Work out an overarching theme for what we want to achieve in advance, and tell people about it

We need to articulate the sort of country we want to see in 2020 and beyond. We need to be clear that our vision of that liberal country where none shall be enslaved by poverty, ignorance and conformity can't be enacted in one Parliament, while setting out how we will work towards it over the next term. In Coalition, we need to make sure that our actions fit in with that theme. While acknowledging that we can't get our own way all of the time, there have been instances where we have not only accepted but embraced policies which we would not have contemplated on our own. One particularly egregious example is the imposition of a minimum income limit before a non EU spouse can be allowed to live in the UK. This policy splits families up and particularly disadvantages British women who are more likely to be taking time out of the labour market if they are caring for children. My view is that we should never have agreed to this in the first place. Having done so, we should have made clear that this was something we would seek to reverse if we were in government on our own. Instead, we have accepted it in principle if not the way it has been implemented in our own recent policy document passed in York in Spring 2014.

In this instance, I can't just blame ministers for something I see as a grave error of policy. I have to share that blame with our party conference, whose sovereign policy making power I also have to accept. There have been other instances, however, where Conference has taken a stand against a particular coalition policy and the ensuing failure of our ministers to change course has caused disquiet and a dangerous disconnect between the leadership and activists. I think particularly of the issues of secret courts and the Bedroom Tax. On the former, the party almost unanimously condemned plans to introduce closed material proceedings in civil trials. The effect is that those suing the government for damages in relation, for example, to being tortured, are unable to see some UK Government evidence, putting them at a severe disadvantage. Six months too late, the first 2015 pre-manifesto themes document, as Liberal Democrat blogger Mark Pack first discovered, included a commitment to find another way:

We will find practical alternatives to the use of closed material proceedings within the justice system, including the provisions of the Justice and Security Act 2013, with the aim of restoring the principle of open justice.[66]

but that could be seen as too little too late.

On the Bedroom Tax, the eagerness of some Liberal Democrat ministers to adopt what the Government's own impact assessment warned would not have the desired effect was particularly disconcerting. Danny Alexander rather too gleefully talked about "bedroom blockers" taking up large social housing. In fact he was referring to a very small number of high-earning trade union officials, but they self-evidently didn't claim Housing Benefit.

3. Keep the party together – avoid the disconnect
The Liberal Democrats need their activists more than any others. We don't have huge funds to play with. We need our people to be out there on the doorsteps telling our story

---

[66] www.markpack.org.uk/45113/david-laws-to-move-conference-motion-proposing-an-end-to-secret-courts

for us because, bluntly, nobody else will. So, keeping your activists onside through the inevitability of taking unpopular decisions in government is vital and something that the party hasn't managed to get right in Scotland or the rest of the UK. In the early days of the UK Coalition, I wrote about the need to avoid this, about how leadership and activists needed to work at their relationship. The old 'walk a mile in each others' shoes' thing works if you do it. Ministers need to understand how activists feel when a policy they don't like is enacted by them. Activists need to understand the various pressures that ministers feel.

Intra-party communications for the first year or so of the coalition were worse than dreadful, reaching a nadir when an email from Simon Hughes as Environment Spokesperson landed in Scottish Members' inboxes days after the devastating Scottish elections. "There's never been a better time to be a Liberal Democrat" it screamed. Sure, we had just scored a significant policy win on the environment but for most Scottish members, the red mist had descended before we realised what the email was about.

There was no improvement a year later. Compare and contrast the different approaches of Nick Clegg and Willie Rennie to disappointing local election results. It was very much keep calm and carry on from Clegg. Willie, on the other hand, rather than merely taking the pulse of the party, synchronised his own heartbeat to it, writing:

"This is a very distressing day. We have lost many, many strong community activists who have stuck up for their area for many long years.

My message to them is this: I am sorry that you have lost out despite your tremendous efforts for the Liberal Democrats and for your communities.

These results should dispel any myth that the Liberal Democrats are only in the coalition for ourselves. We never were. It has always been about doing the right thing for the fortunes of the country.[67]

Ministers need to at least show that they remember that the party exists. They shouldn't make announcements about what our policy will be without proper consultation. Nor should they agree to new legislation outside the Coalition Agreement which they should know the party would instinctively, and rightly, oppose. In fact, they shouldn't agree any such legislation without some sort of consultation.

4. Get everyone on the same page before agreeing to new legislation

In April 2012, Nick Clegg announced support for new legislation which would force internet service providers to store data about which websites we had visited, and who had sent messages via social media to whom. Experts in the party who understand the technology quickly realised that this legislation posed a huge threat to our civil liberties for very little gain in security. They knew, for example, that it was impossible to separate the timing of the message from the actual content.

To their credit, the leadership agreed to a conference call between a special adviser and several Liberal Democrat bloggers which took place on Tuesday 3 April. It's fair to say that this was quite an angry call. However, it kick-started the ultimate withdrawal of Liberal Democrat support for the measure. Clegg ensured that the legislation was brought forward only in draft form so that it was subjected to additional scrutiny. When the Parliamentary Committee rejected the legislation, he immediately, to Theresa May's fury, accepted their points.

---

[67] http://carons-musings.blogspot.co.uk/2012/05/nick-get-new-ghost-writer-with-some.html

However, if he had consulted even just one or two experts in the party before agreeing to the plan, he could have put his foot down from the start. There is an argument that the way it worked out was actually advantageous for the Liberal Democrats. It is much more difficult to paint the Liberal Democrats as soft on crime when it is an influential parliamentary committee which has pointed out the flaws in the legislation. That said, it would have been better if Clegg had pushed for a draft bill in the first place and reserved judgment until the Committee reported. Because he initially accepted the principles of the legislation, the party lost a bit of faith in his instincts on these crucial matters. An earlier engagement with the party might have avoided or lessened the anger directed at him in the wake of the European election results.

5. Have a protocol for negotiating things outside the Coalition Agreement

Related to this is the issue of how you deal with things that come up during your term of office that are not referred to in your Coalition Agreement. The Liberal Democrats and Labour in Scotland had procedures for this hardwired into their partnership. The Conservatives and Liberal Democrats at Westminster did not. There has been a significant difference of approach between the two governments. At Westminster, there has been more of a tendency to trade policies so that the Liberal Democrats get some things, the Conservatives get others. Vince Cable spoke about the "messy compromises" that had to be made in Coalition Government at the Social Liberal Forum Conference in 2014, citing the hiking of Industrial Tribunal fees as an example. Jim Wallace as Deputy First Minister in Scotland, in contrast, was more careful about negotiating every single point. In 2011, he told *Holyrood* magazine how he and First Minister Jack McConnell used a thesaurus during some late night negotiations on planning law to find a form of words which would be acceptable to both parties.

When dealing with those issues which crop up for every government, though, care must be taken to ensure that Liberal Democrats don't sound too comfortable with power and the establishment.

6. Never, ever sound like the establishment – there is more that needs to be changed

The moment when Liberal Democrat heads went down in the 2014 European election was when Nick Clegg said, during this second debate with Nigel Farage, that the European Union would be much the same in 10 years' time as it was today. He lost a prime opportunity to say what Liberal Democrats thought was wrong with the EU and how we would fix it and by doing so made it look like we favoured the status quo.

The tragedy is that Nick has actually been arguing, probably more than any other leader, for specific, meaningful reform of the EU for longer than any other British political leader. I remember him talking at a dinner in the East Midlands back in 1998 with great passion about how blinkered the institutions of the EU could be.

The Liberal Democrats are by nature a radical, insurgent party, in government or out of it. We always need to be seen to be standing up to the vested interests who want to keep things as they are. There is much more to be done to make our society genuinely free and fair than can be accomplished in any one term of office and that's why we need to make time amidst the business of running the country that we keep refreshing and developing our policies to fit the changing needs of our society.

7. Work out the next steps for the next term – don't run out of steam

Given recent history, an antipathy towards presenting radical policies might be understandable but it would be very unwise to go into the election with a set of timid, pale ideas that grabbed nobody's heart. So far, the main ideas to come out of the party's manifesto process are an annual Carer's Bonus, introducing higher Council Tax bands for houses worth over £2 million and further raising the tax threshold to minimum wage level. It's all very worthy, but it's merely tinkering at the edges.

I have long said that the most important thing any government can do is sort out the amount and quality of affordable housing. Nick Clegg recognises that we need to build more houses and has come up with a welcome plan for five new garden cities. However, that's simply not enough. In his 2014 Beveridge Lecture, Tim Farron said that we need to be far more radical, calling for active, ambitious liberal government to ensure infrastructure improvements and, crucially, commit to creating 3 million new homes during the next Parliament, using a combination of abolishing the right to buy, government guarantees and lifting the cap on borrowing requirements for housing associations. His remarks have been criticised for lack of substance but in fact his proposals came out of careful work with experts in the field and housing associations themselves.

As a party we need to constantly evaluate what our society needs and will need in the future. Then we need to communicate it in a way that tugs at people's heart strings.

8. Campaign with your heart

Fancy social media infographics telling the world how many apprenticeships we have created or who many million jobs we've been responsible for is unlikely to win us votes. It's personal experiences of how our ideas in action have benefitted people that will make people instinctively feel that we get it, that we understand the realities of their lives and have the right ideas to help them.

Liberal Democrats also need to be much better at rebuttal. If you listen to many elements of the media, you would think that we'd privatised the NHS and not done the slightest thing to help the poorest in our society. We need to be better at taking on those arguments. The NHS is still free at the point of use. We have put billions into supporting disadvantaged children in school and already the results are showing increases in attainment, particularly amongst BAME children. The Scottish party has been successful in persuading the Scottish Government to follow Westminster's lead in several areas, particularly early years childcare and free school meals, but we need to make sure that the public don't forget about this.

There can be no coincidence that when the Liberal Democrats were in coalition at Holyrood, civil liberties in Scotland were much stronger than south of the border. Think much more robust freedom of information vs London Labour's identity database. Funnily enough, when the Liberal Democrats are in coalition at Westminster, the UK Government's record on civil liberties is much stronger than the Scottish Government's. Armed police on the streets of the Highlands, over-used, unregulated stop and search, prison conditions, most notably lack of mental health support all provide opportunities for us to campaign with our hearts and show why we are needed. It's important that over the next two years we take up that challenge.

After the Coalition –
Future Challenges to Liberalism

Nigel Lindsay

A key insight of Liberals is that the power of the state – wherever it is located, from supra-national to local level – can be harnessed for the benefit of the poor and those most disadvantaged in society. With an optimistic view of the world and a strong belief in the idea of progress, Liberals have seen the use of political power as central to creating the conditions in which self-realization is possible for all. Taking political liberty as a foundation, Liberals in government and in opposition – whether national or local – have tended to seek ways of ensuring that such liberty is valid; that is, capable of use. As Nigel Dower puts it earlier in this book, liberty is valuable only "if the conditions are in place for the effective exercise of liberty".

Liberals in elected positions and in government have shown over many years how people can be raised up and enabled to fulfil themselves by putting in place structures which overcome disadvantage. From the introduction of National Insurance and Old Age Pensions by Asquith and Lloyd George, through the development of the welfare state and the move to a national health service following the report of the Liberal MP Sir William Beveridge, to the provision of free personal care for the elderly and free university tuition for the young introduced by Liberal Democrats in the Scottish Government, our party has used legislative power and government resource to make freedom useful for citizens. Liberals in local government have similarly used resources and powers to improve quality of life and increase life expectancy for the poorest by means such as the provision of clean water and improving air quality.

It is important to note in passing that, though a similar approach is claimed by the Labour Party, they have failed with a few exceptions to deliver such radical change. This has been partly because of an innate centralising tendency that militates against individual freedom and self-realization, and partly because a well-meaning emphasis on the welfare of particular social groups has led them to bureaucratic, expensive, and often unworkable mechanisms for rectifying individual disadvantage. It follows that legislative change, supporting people to become what they want, is likely to be pushed forward only by Liberals, or by Liberals in coalition with another party keen to follow a similar agenda.

This insight, central to Liberalism, has been damaged since 2010 by association with a party that has a much less sophisticated notion of liberty, and implementation by the coalition of policies that have at times hindered rather than helped people with the fewest resources to make the most of themselves. Adverse change to the benefits system, weakening of the NHS in England, and a shift from progressive taxation to VAT, are some of the factors that have together started to undo many of the great advances made by Liberals in the 20th century. Our party, which voters once identified clearly with an agenda of reform and social justice, has lost much of the trust it had on these issues. The Party will need to work hard, once the coalition has ended, to persuade voters that it is still capable of radical action to help the least well-off to meet their aspirations.

A start can be made by abandoning the facile rhetoric of the last few years, which claims we have moved from being a party of protest to a party of government. This is a false dichotomy if ever there was one, and it is in any case inaccurate. Liberals had been in government long before 2010: in coalition with the Labour Party in Scotland, and in Wales as Ross Finnie has pointed out elsewhere in this book. He should know. He was a LibDem Minister well before any of the present ones. Liberals have also played a crucial role as the governing party in Liverpool, Aberdeen, Hull, Newcastle, Edinburgh, and countless other local authorities over the past forty years. So it is grossly inaccurate, anywhere other than at Westminster, to claim that Liberals have only recently become a party of government.

Nor were Liberals ever a party of protest. The Liberal Party and later the Liberals Democrats have been over the years a fertile source of new and workable ideas on how Britain should be governed. It is instructive to look back at Liberal Party manifestoes from the 1960s and 1970s, and to realise how many of the ideas in them have been implemented over the years, without the presence of any Liberal ministers in national government. A quick look at the Liberal manifesto for the first 1974 general election shows Liberals pressing for devolution to Scotland and Wales (as David Steel points out elsewhere in this book); a national minimum wage; the introduction of housing benefit; the establishment of Small Claims Courts; and the integration of Universities, polytechnics, and colleges of education. All these proposals were opposed and even ridiculed by "parties of government". But all of them passed into law before any Liberal Democrat was a minister in Whitehall! These ideas, developed by Liberal activists who saw need, analysed it, and came up with new and radical solutions, were patiently argued by Liberal MPs and councillors, and eventually put into effect by other parties. The Liberal Party certainly benefited at times from so-called protest votes. The Labour and Conservative Parties also benefit from protest votes at times when they are in opposition. But ours was never a "party of protest".

Jo Grimond (whose Liberalism is ably described by Willis Pickard in another chapter) had useful advice on these matters. He said that Liberals are on the side of the governed rather than the government. This is a succinct way of encapsulating the important truth that the point of having power is to use it for the benefit of those who are powerless. In other words, there would be no useful and Liberal achievement in being a junior minister who spends days signing off uncontroversial items of secondary legislation while the ministry itself is engaged on, say, unfair and ill-researched changes to the benefits system. Liberals should be in government to use political power for those who have none, not to be glorified administrators

This should not obscure the fact that some useful advances were made by Liberal Democrats in the Coalition, particularly in its first year or two. As has been mentioned elsewhere in this book, the pension reforms guided by Steve Webb and the welcome abandonment of Labour's planned introduction of identity cards are thoroughly praiseworthy. Unfortunately, the latter contribution to protection of civil rights has been overshadowed by more recent agreements, to extend the use of secret courts and to widen powers to intercept and store private communications. Oddly, though, one of the Liberal Democrat actions in Westminster this year which had real potential to bring about positive change in the future was not any ministerial decision, but Michael Moore's private member's bill on overseas aid. And I find it disappointing that not one of the great offices of state has been held by a Liberal Democrat under the coalition, and that Liberal Democrats in government have sometimes allowed themselves to be used as cover for the implementation of thoroughly nasty Conservative ideas.

A significant challenge for Liberal Democrats in the years after the coalition will therefore be to rediscover how to link our core principles with our political actions. This will be necessary whether we are in government or in opposition. How effectively we can do it will determine how quickly we regain the trust of voters. This, though, may be the least of the challenges facing Liberalism over the next decade or two.

If I am correct in stating that the use of political power is central to the Liberal way of creating the conditions in which self-realization is possible for all, then there are some very serious threats to the possibility of governments using power for this purpose. They are not far away. Among them are three that we need to consider urgently. The first is that the political power of governments is being eclipsed by the power of large international corporations. The second is the ever-increasing globalisation of what we ironically call financial services, and the mass movement of money by financial institutions and hedge fund speculators, over which governments have little control. The third is the mass movement of people fleeing from despotic and incompetent regimes, which is certain to have a substantial impact on all parts of Europe over the next decade or two. Let us look briefly at each of these in turn.

If international corporations have larger budgets and greater power than the governments that seek to regulate them on behalf of the people, then injustices are almost bound to occur. The power that the largest oil companies exercise over states has been documented over many years. When the interests of governments are dwarfed by the power of oil interests, how can they call a halt to exploration in sensitive areas, or impose tax regimes that the oil companies consider burdensome or oppose fracking? How much influence is exerted over foreign policy towards oil-rich areas? And how can pricing cartels and structures be held to account? None of this is new, but governments have yet to find an effective way of resisting the will of major oil companies.

More recently, we have seen banks develop an international reach and a way of doing business globally that is hard for governments to control effectively. Twenty years ago, RBS and Bank of Scotland were successful and ambitious Scottish banks with their eyes on a wider UK market. By 2008 they had become enmeshed with subsidiaries, some overseas, which domestic regulators were not able to control and which brought them down. Insult was added to injury when, after taxpayers in the shape of the government rescued one of these banks, it employed its own lobbyists to work for what management saw as its own interests, against the decisions being made by the ministers who spoke for its owners. It is instructive to note that, in spite of all the evidence of malpractice in UK banks including manipulation of the LIBOR rate, of the gold rate, and of foreign exchange rates, all of which acted against customer interests and the common good, not one British banker has yet been jailed. That, more than almost anything, shows how powerful banks have become.

"Big Pharma" similarly operates now on a global scale. The 2014 failure of Pfizer's takeover bid for Astra Zeneca happened not because the UK government stepped in to halt the takeover (it didn't) but because the markets were not convinced. And it is particularly relevant to ask whether regulators knew of or had any powers to control the corrupt practices alleged against GSK in China. Here is another industry largely beyond the control of government.

The list goes on. Media companies are another example. Google and Amazon (for instance) have become so powerful that they seem able to dictate the tax regimes of sovereign states within the EU, such as Ireland and Luxembourg. News International (as it used to be known) has been shown to operate in ways that many would judge to be against the public interest. It has been a difficult and expensive business for the public to call any of this to account. That such power is greater than that of governments is amply illustrated by the way in which high-ranking ministers in both the Labour and Conservative parties from Tony Blair onwards, have seemed keen to follow the agenda of senior News International figures. It has been left to courageous back-benchers such as Tom Watson to question what has been going on.

All of this is well-known and perhaps inevitable. But it does pose awkward questions for Liberals. If we believe in using the power of the state to make it easier for citizens to realise their aspirations, what do we do if the state itself is controlled or heavily influenced by corporations whose aims are not concurrent with this? How can we create the conditions in which liberty exists and can be made valid, when interests more powerful than the government we hope to form are opposing action of this sort?

Deregulation of financial markets in the USA, which was then copied by the UK, and in particular the repeal of 80-year-old legislation regulating US banks in the late 1990s, led to consequences which should have been foreseen. I have already alluded to how British banks were brought low by ill-advised and little-understood investments in the US housing market which even their own directors did not understand. These difficulties were not prevented by regulators and the government, because neither had the power or adequate understanding of what was happening, and because banks were able to invest more or less freely in whatever jurisdiction they chose.

Similarly, we have seen over the last quarter century how a currency can be brought low or devalued simply at the whim of investors moving huge amounts of money from one country to another. Sometimes this is done with political intent, sometimes without, but it always has a political effect. The facility to do this was created by those who speak of free markets that are in reality only free for the very rich but it is not a facility that is likely to be removed any time soon. Rather, we are likely to see more of it. Does it operate in the public interest? Does it contribute to the well-being of ordinary citizens in this country or abroad? If not, again Liberals need to question how their fundamental purpose is compromised by those in the money markets who seem able to exert far more power than does any government. What is the point of getting Liberals into government, if they are constrained from action by bodies whose power exceeds that of a democratic mandate?

One answer might be: in order to create greater control by institutions representing the general interest. Control in this sense must mean more than regulation. It should include effective inspection, agreed and enforceable standards of ethics, and the provision of speedy and effective remedies These needs are perhaps not so different from those demanded by John the Common Weal in that great 16th century Scots drama *Ane Satyre of the Thrie Estaitis* but, as in those times, it will require an authority with extraordinary courage as well as power to implement them

The increasing freedom with which huge levels of funds are transferred rapidly around the world has a resonance with the apparently different but actually related phenomenon of the mass movement of people from country to country and continent to continent. Zones of conflict have always led to movement of refugees into neighbouring countries but the last sixty years may come to be seen as a period of relative population stability. The movement of people across Africa and towards Europe may have its roots in oppression and economic hardship in states such as Eritrea and Nigeria. The instability caused by the disastrous western interventions in Iraq and Libya, and by the civil war in Syria, are also significant contributory factors.

The urgent need to reach Europe that is felt by the travellers is shown by the desperate dangers they face. They know they face the risk of dying in the intense heat of a journey across the Sahara clinging onto the side of a lorry. They know that if they fall off, no-one will return to save them. They will be aware of the fate of those who attempt to make even the shortest journeys across the Mediterranean, with scores having died from asphyxiation, and hundreds by drowning in the last year alone. And they know that if they arrive in Malta or Lampedusa, they will be confined in camps with few facilities, often for a year or more.

No Liberal can observe these tragedies without feeling anger at the events which cause them, and compassion for those who take such risks under the most extreme of stresses. With our international outlook, Liberals will agree that these are not problems simply for the governments of Italy and Malta. We deplore the shameful lack of understanding or human sympathy shown by UKIP's leaders, and we are uneasy about a government and opposition that prefer to look the other way. We have a natural desire to help those caught up in these situations, and we search for ways to tackle the root cause of these migrations, none of which are motivated by anything other than necessity.

Yet as Liberals we also seek the maintenance of the Liberal values that still underlie the British state, and recognise that these may be compromised by the rapid arrival of new populations which do not share a commitment to these values. The problem arises in two ways: first, from the antagonism to visible members of an immigrant population that seems to be so easily stirred up by the parties of the right – an antagonism that causes some people very quickly to forsake the liberal values which they have tacitly accepted in the past. Second, different cultural or religious beliefs may be fairly starkly at variance with Liberal values – issues for instance concerning forced marriages, female genital mutilation, the status and education of women generally, and perhaps wider issues involving education. Indeed, as other contributors to this book have noted, these values and the authority of elected government itself may sometimes be challenged by faith groups which put belief systems above democratic legitimacy. How far freedom of speech and action in such matters extends in the liberal democracy for which we stand remains a tortuous and challenging question.

With caveats about such difficult matters, Liberals recognise that their stress on self-realization cannot be separated from their emphasis on internationalism. Liberty, and the conditions that make it useful, are not just for citizens of one country. They are for everyone. This may mean some adjustments of our expectations, and a realization that we only enjoy our present wealth and stability at the cost of the many millions who do not. Joseph Chamberlain, while still representing Birmingham as an Advanced Radical and before his later political recidivism, shocked his electors 130 years ago by asking what ransom property should pay for its security. As a 19th century nonconformist he used the word "ransom" with its theological rather than criminal overtones. Understood in that way, his question may still shock some but it has some relevance to the rights, liberties and property we now enjoy while the majority of the world's population has no such privileges. A similar point was made later by that most Liberal of Liberal Prime Ministers, Sir Henry Campbell-Bannerman, when he said "It is not power, nor glory, nor wealth, that exalteth a nation, but righteousness, justice, and freedom".

Ross Finnie, in his contribution to this book, has eloquently set out in the context of coalitions, the need for a party approaching government to be clear about the main political aims it wishes to achieve. I believe it is equally important for any party seeking to govern or participate in government to have a clear understanding of the context in which government will operate over the next ten or more years, and to be acutely aware of the likely obstacles to delivery of its programme, the possible challenges to its purposes, and the most effective ways in which these can be overcome.

As Liberals, we tend to analyse and react to present conditions when developing policy. My task in this short contribution has been to attempt to show that this is no longer good enough and that we now need to grasp clearly the forces that will be at work to oppose the actions of any future government, whether or not it is influenced by our party. I am acutely aware that I have provided more questions than answers, but hope this may act as a starting point for further discussion and thought.

Geographic Justice in a Global Age

The Highlands and Islands in an Age of Globalism

Kate Stephen

There's a map of Scotland from 1673 on which the Inner and Outer Hebrides are oversized. Firths and bays along the west coast are portrayed in intricate detail. Ireland is a stone's throw away and Edinburgh is a barely decipherable dot. Scotland's 'central belt' in those days was based on the marine thoroughfare from the Minch to the Irish Sea. No-one would have called us remote then! But over the following three and a half centuries, aided by the introduction of steam liners, roads, and railways, the people and power drifted away. What we have now are lots of small, scattered communities, an ageing population and patchy broadband. The area is breathtakingly beautiful but as the Russian fisherman from Bill Forsyth's film *Local Hero* says, "You can't eat scenery".

Life in the Highlands is undeniably good in world terms. We live at peace with our neighbours and there are consistently low levels of crime. We enjoy clean air and good quality food. Opportunities and freedoms for every citizen are enshrined in legislation. But it would be naive and dishonest to suggest that every citizen feels safe and fulfilled. Not everyone can afford to maintain a healthy diet.

181

And not everyone is able to say that they are not discriminated against even subtly because of their gender, ethnicity, family background, accent, sexual orientation, caring responsibility, or disability.

It can be possible to live a simple life, far away from the temptations of John Lewis and Marks and Spencer. The 'must have' fashion item in the Highlands and Islands is a waterproof, fleece-lined jacket. But the absence of 'things' is not always a lifestyle choice. Poverty is exacerbated by low pay, seasonal employment, high costs of travel to work, and a shortage of quality, affordable housing to rent.

Although we don't usually grab the headlines with our statistics for deprivation, there are pockets of poor health and poverty, often hidden beneath the surface of what appears to be a rural idyll. And there are both new challenges and new opportunities for the Highlands and Islands in a global age: the distance from larger markets and from services, the potential of the "brand" in tourism (particularly cultural tourism perhaps, as the success of the Gaelic College on Skye indicates), different economic and employment opportunities as tidal power and other technologies take off. But the Highlands and Islands need a vision, an optimism and a confidence which has been undermined by population decline and withdrawal.

With the Scottish referendum and the prospect of an EU in-out referendum these are interesting times. Folk are being asked to make stark choices and it has generated some reflection and debate about what matters to us and what we want our country to be like. This chapter is written from this context and from a Highland perspective. Underlying the chapter is a question; "in an age of globalisation and austerity, what is required of government to help peripheral, rural areas adapt to survive?"

Spatial Inequality

In a geographical area like the Highlands and Islands, the main additional challenge is spatial inequality. This comes in the form of the increasing costs of delivering services to small, scattered communities with ageing populations, and the higher cost of goods, not least fuel. Young people drift south to urban centres for education and employment (and a more varied night life!). There is a lack of critical mass to allow economies of scale. We are peripheral in a London-centric UK and a Brussels-centric EU – and indeed in an Edinburgh-centric Scotland. Long before the Union with England and even up to the beginning of the 19th century, the Highlands and the Lowlands of Scotland were very different – and often antagonistic – places, with different language, culture and societies.

Such thoughts lay behind the creation of the University of the Highlands and Islands (awarded University status in 2011) which has the potential to provide intellectual stimulus to creative thinking about the Region, to look at economic development, planning and tourism successes in other countries and their relevance to us. The University already offers an MSc in Sustainable Rural Development and houses an Economic Intelligence Unit focused on the economy of the Highlands and Islands.

The University, of course, fulfils a variety of functions but, in this context, I believe there would be great advantage in something like a Highlands and Islands Economic Institute which was able to access appropriate funding from government or trust sources to fulfil a pivotal role in cutting edge research in this area – a thinktank for reinventing the economy and the future of the Highlands and islands. It is relevant to recall that the region once supported a much larger population. Such a thinktank might be based on a consortium between UHI and the other Universities such as

Aberdeen or Glasgow which provide research and teaching in relevant areas.

And, if the Universities can be the ideas-machine for the area, then we need the political and administrative institutions to implement the ideas. The Convention of the Highlands and Islands is a body meeting twice yearly which comprises principally the region's Parliamentarians, the local authorities and other public bodies active in the area meeting with Scottish and UK Ministers. I believe it could have much more significance than it does presently – could it, for example, have devolved to it, as the historian and former Chair of Highlands and Islands Enterprise, Professor Jim Hunter suggested, a proportion of the powers which the Scottish Parliament has? Or is there wider resonance in the call from the Islands representatives for substantial devolution of powers to them? Or is the City Deal model, developed by the Coalition government for England and the subject of a 20 year £1,000billion deal for Greater Glasgow something which could be adapted for use in the Highlands and Islands? However it is done, there is a stark need for the region to have more direct and consolidated powers to shape and improve its own future.

Rural Health

Of all the social inequalities in today's United Kingdom, one of the most disturbing is in health. The disparity in longevity of life, especially in men from different data-zones, is appalling. Of all the differences between rich and poor, the result of health inequality is to be deprived of life itself. In the Highlands and Islands in the past, we have had quite a few 'Dr Finlay' types. Their case books were so small they could afford to give personal attention and time to patients. People actually 'felt' cared for. Now our poor health is exacerbated by the 'tyranny of distance' which makes accessing specialist health services difficult. Problems are compounded by recruitment difficulties to specialist posts (though why people don't want to come here to live and work is beyond me!).

The impact of illness and disability is more difficult to overcome when treatments are distant and support is scarce. These factors are not always accounted for in welfare reform. It is easier for rural people to fall though the crack between ineligibility for Job Seekers Allowance or for Personal Independence Payment.

Financial hardship results from the costs and inconvenience of travel to sign on and lack of access to online information and applications. This contributes to rural disadvantage. The current Westminster incentives to lure/push people out of benefits dependency into work don't always fit well in remote, rural areas. No wonder many feel there is no option but to move south. We need alternative models, or at least sufficiently flexible approaches that can adapt to suit circumstances in the Highlands and Islands as well as the rest of the UK.

Recruitment

Recruitment to the health and social care sector and the tourism and hospitality industry face similar challenges. In health, recruitment to specialised posts is an on-going challenge in the Highlands and Islands. As a result there can be loss of quality in service delivery and increase in cost from temporary and locum cover. If this problem remains unaddressed, there will be a resultant centralisation of health services and a decrease in the options for healthcare locally.

We have long given up hope of recruiting from within Scotland. Currently, the recruitment net is flung to the furthermost parts of Europe in order to catch a consultant! But despite these efforts, posts remain unfilled. In the tourist industry the situation is similar. If you pop in for a cuppa, a nip, or a bite at a scenic hotel or café in the

Highlands and Islands, the likelihood is you'll not be served by someone with a local accent.

Without people coming here to work we would not sustain our economy or maintain our services. And increasingly our demography points to an ageing population with not enough babies being born to provide a tax-paying workforce to sustain it. We need younger families and we need immigrants from outwith the area. In other parts of the UK, there is less need for an external supply of workers. This is where we have a mismatch. While we desperately try to attract people of whatever nationality to the Highlands and Islands, the Westminster government (whatever its political composition) is under pressure to introduce policies that deter immigration.

But it will probably be immigration from elsewhere in Britain that is most important. The attraction to people with family connections or ancestry in the Highlands and the western and northern isles is potentially strong, providing there are job or business opportunities for them.

A different approach is required to meet the challenges of recruitment in the Highlands and Islands. In part, this may incorporate sponsorship of or grants to local individuals for training and education in the areas where we have gaps linked to guarantees of employment on graduation. They do this in Japan for rural general practitioners with some success.

Sponsorship programmes could be designed to meet gaps expected in 5 years' time. But to meet immediate need, a tax reimbursement scheme which provides an incentive for employers and foreign employees could be used to help attract highly skilled immigrants. This exists in the Netherlands and is targeted specifically for sectors and jobs in which recruitment is problematic.

Although the Netherlands is very different to the UK in terms of density, they too have a northern territory (Friesland) which looks and sounds different from the rest of the country. There is potential for some of the ideas they have generated in response to these differences to inform Westminster and Holyrood policies to better suit the Highlands and Islands, such as employment benefit. In rural areas, where full employment is not always possible throughout the year, a more flexible approach to benefits could provide increased stability. Where there are fragile rural communities heavily reliant on tourism, an unemployment benefit akin to that in the Netherlands would support seasonally unemployed people throughout the closed season. Their benefit gives people 75% of their last earned wage for the first two months. Eligibility is based on a minimum of 26 weeks employment out of the 36 weeks prior to the first day of unemployment and evidence of job searching is required.

In a way, such schemes are the obverse of London weightings in pay and allowances which are designed to meet similar challenges caused by population density rather than sparsity in the capital. They are equally justified – if not more so.

Employment

In terms of job creation, a different approach is also required. Managers from urban centres tend to focus activity in the Highlands and Islands during the half of the year which has more light and better weather. This makes complete sense from their perspective in avoiding icy road conditions and cancelled ferries and planes.

But, from a local perspective, the winter is the best time for project work, consultations and information events – that is when local people have time. In the spring and summer, there are activities such as lambing; sheep dipping; cutting peats, turning them and taking them in; visitors; gatherings, shows and fetes; as well as jobs in hospitality and tourism. Increased awareness about the rural yearly life cycle could result in better timing of temporary posts and short-term contracts which could complement rather than complete with existing commitments.

As well as a different approach from the public sector in regard to job creation, there is huge potential for small and medium private enterprises. The Federation of Small Business's report *Back to Work, the role of small businesses in employment and enterprise* states that older workers (over retirement age), younger workers (16-24 years), and rural workers are more likely to be employed in small or medium businesses. The report suggests that "in small firms there is less formality, more fluidity and greater flexibility in the employment relationship" which is of benefit not just for rural people but for those who struggle to enter, re-enter or remain in employment. It further suggests that the inherent flexibility of small firms is a key factor in their ability to create jobs. Similar to the point made earlier about the different approaches required for rural areas, the report states that "different approaches are needed for small and large firms". There is a clear parallel between the response required to needs of small firms and the needs of rural and remote areas.

Transport

Transport links and services are fundamental to the Highlands and Islands. The Coalition government has focused with some success on the issue of petrol prices in the Highlands, while the Scottish Government, under several administrations, have increasingly supported life-line links to the islands. Roads, ferries, buses, trains, canals are the arteries of the region – but they have been decaying arteries as bus services are in particular decline. Again this is an area for new thinking which can build on experience in Scandinavia and elsewhere, equally challenged by remoteness, rurality – and weather! The Skye Bridge has played a major part in helping develop the island – and there are opportunities elsewhere to link some of the islands by bridges.

This is not an issue with easy answers but tourism and transport are catalysts which can mutually support the achievement of critical mass and more viable services and facilities.

Co-production

In the public sector, there is potential for a co-production approach to realise some of the fluidity and flexibility enjoyed by SMEs . In the context of a global financial crisis and the subsequent reduction in public sector budgets, rural areas such as the Highlands and Islands are under increased threat. As various public services are slimmed down or cut altogether, fragile rural areas are disproportionately affected – especially as a result of job losses in public administration and the knock on effect on local businesses.

Ineffective community planning which allows individual services to act (and cut) as if in isolation can result in fragile communities becoming either expensively problematic or unsustainable. This fragility results in and is exacerbated by the global phenomenon of population shift from rural to urban, both between regions and also within local areas.

A further challenge exists where, as a result of a cultural expectation that the state will provide for us, individuals and communities become angry when they feel the state is not performing satisfactorily or is negating to perform some basic duties. Learned dependency can make individuals, and our communities, less resilient. But the sledgehammer-like effect of cuts to rural services doesn't always have to result in a culture of helplessness and despondency. Where public services are under threat, there is an opportunity to take a fresh look at how we can do things differently to be more effective. Co-production is an approach which provides the flexibility to allow this to happen.

Over recent times, as some communities have become frustrated with the lack of state action on matters which they care about, they have increasingly taken on more themselves. Activity around community land and asset ownership, development of amenities and even the taking over of service delivery has become increasingly common. Huge leaps have been taken by communities across the country, including small rural communities in the Highlands and Islands: Applecross, Assynt, Eigg, Gigha, Glenurquhart and Tongue to name but a few. But despite the policy rhetoric (Community Empowerment (Scotland) Bill, 2014; "Doing with, not to", NES / SCDC, 2011; JIT's "Co-production of health and wellbeing in Scotland", 2012), levels of inertia in resisting change are stymieing progress.

The Gaelic phrase "tachraidh na daoine, ach cha tachair na cnuic" (translated "men will meet, but the hills will not") helps to focus the mind on what can and cannot be changed. There are inescapable realities faced by residents in the Highlands and Islands which will remain, whoever governs and wherever they govern from.

There is no point in trying to change the economy of the Highlands to simulate the South of England or the Central Belt of Scotland and, it follows that an economic policy that fits one area is unlikely to fit the other. Instead, the challenges we face should be acknowledged and national policies should either be developed at a federal or regional level or at least should be adaptable to fit regional circumstances.

We need flexibility on the part of government to respond to individual regions instead of having a blanket policy for the whole UK. It is important to avoid the tendency to assume there is homogeneity. It is crucial that recognition of local and regional differences is integral in policy development. Where Federalism is an obvious structure which would provide the flexibility needed, I suggest it should be supplemented by 'co-production'.

The word co-production is used to describe a shift in mind set from paternalistic service delivery to a partnership of equals (including community and customers) who work together. The shift is away from top down models towards local identification of priorities and local development of solutions.

Co-production is localism in practice. It involves the pragmatic passing of power to the people. Instead of top-down cuts, it allows local public services to be more efficient. There is less waste and more shared and creative use of local assets. There is more potential for local development of solutions to local problems. This can extend from social care to transport, from energy production to housing. In terms of Liberal principles, co-production supports the notion of responsibility, not just for individuals but at community level. Furthermore, it fits seamlessly with the notion of case-by-case solutions, sensitive to context, which Ben Colburn argues for in *The Little Yellow Book*.

Political Context

The Highlands and Islands are similar to many other regions in that it is tempting to ascribe certain characteristics to its inhabitants. Some favourite generic Highland personality traits would include: unassuming; thrawn; frugal at home but generously hospitable; at times driven by a Calvinistic work ethic, at other times refraining from doing today what could be put off till tomorrow; a composed demeanour with deep regret and hurt revealed only if aided by a nip or the gospel. But the reality today is as it has always been; a mix of different types of people and personality types. And, this includes a mix of political views.

For two centuries, much of the Highlands have normally been represented in Westminster by Liberals. The Liberals were popular both because they represented the social and religious concerns of the area, and also because they reflected and advocated the priorities of the people – not just in the redistribution of land, but in arguing for basic provision such as minimum wage and pensions. They were long associated with the vital land issue, particularly with the passing of the Crofters' Holdings (Scotland) Act in 1886.

In more recent times, the three Westminster Highland constituencies have returned Liberal Democrat MPs for decades with Charles Kennedy MP holding his seat for over thirty years. But, there are no laurels to rest upon.

In the Scottish Parliament, the picture is now very different. The SNP represents all three seats, two of which were lost by the Lib Dems at the last election. The 2014 European elections surprised many when over 10% of the Scottish vote went to UKIP. The challenge for Liberal Democrats is clear. Liberalism is a political tradition in which I take some pride. I look forward to the day when I can take equal pride in the legacy we now pave as Liberal Democrats. For this to happen, I believe we need to "develop and give meaning to the idea of localism", as Robert Brown argued in *The Little Yellow Book*. Not in a Tory-like, top-down Big Society mantra but in a genuine move to empower people and local communities.

Furthermore, the flexibility to target efforts such as sponsorship, grants and tax schemes in response to local challenges could also apply to other areas within the UK. In trying to make a special case for the Highlands and Islands, others would benefit from the precedent of local responsiveness.

Liberalism rather than Nationalism (whether of the SNP or the UKIP variety) has been the natural expression of these hardy and independent communities for generations. With a redeveloped commitment to local power and local answers sitting alongside great traditional Liberal principles, I believe Liberal Democrats will be well placed to be again the political voice of the Highlands and Islands.

London versus the Rest

Tony Hughes

As we approach the 2015 General Election, it seems that hardly a day passes without some mention of the growing economic divide between London and the South East and the remainder of the United Kingdom.

Data gathered in 2013 by the Centre for Cities shows that the capital was responsible for four out of every five new jobs created in the private sector between 2010 and 2012.[68] More recently, research by the Halifax Building Society has found that house prices in Kensington and Chelsea are now more than ten times higher on a like-for-like, average cost per square metre, basis than those in Wishaw, Lanark, Greenock, Airdrie and Kilmarnock.[69]

All political parties are now proposing measures to address this 'problem'. These range from controlling immigration to building HS2, with previously-tried interventions such as relocating administrative functions outwith London and grant-aiding transport infrastructure and housing development in the UK's regional cities once again on the agenda.

---

[68] The Guardian, Monday 27 January 2014
[69] Halifax Building Society, June 2014

But is London's dominance necessarily a problem? Boris Johnson, as Mayor of London, has frequently argued that London's dominance as a world city is good for UK plc and that London's increasing prosperity will eventually filter through to the remainder of the UK. This may be true but, in the meantime, the under-performance of much of the UK's economy represents a significant waste of resources in terms of both unemployed labour and the resulting social welfare costs.

Concerns over the economic divide between the north and south of the UK are nothing new. The run-down of heavy industry in the UK which followed the end of the Second World War disproportionately affected those living in the north of the UK where much of the UK's coal, steel and shipbuilding industries were located. This was followed in the latter part of the twentieth century by a shift from manufacturing to service industry, which again favoured those living and working in southern Britain.

What is different as the country emerges from the current recession is that the economic recovery is much more pronounced in London and its immediate hinterland than anywhere else in the UK. This is bad news not only for those living outwith London and the south east but also for Londoners. With house prices in London rising more rapidly than elsewhere in Britain, home ownership in London is currently unthinkable for many without a foot already on the property ladder. Moreover, the current rate of house-price inflation in London is exacerbating the capital's housing shortage as property is purchased increasingly by non-residents as an investment instead of a home and, in extreme cases, remains unoccupied.

It would therefore appear advantageous to all, other than London's property speculators, to reduce the differential between London property prices and those elsewhere in the UK. But how is this to be achieved? Not, I would suggest, by re-visiting many of the interventionist policies tried previously.

The principal reason for the high cost of London housing is a shortage of supply. This is not a new phenomenon and the fact that it is such a prominent problem today must be due, at least in part, to the inefficacy of previous attempts to address it. These attempts fall into two categories: either to increase the supply of affordable London housing or to reduce the number of people seeking to live in London. They include the payment of 'London weighting allowances', the development of Garden Cities, London 'overspill' housing schemes in the Home Counties and the enforced movement of jobs to areas of high unemployment.

London skills shortage and lack of essential workers is, in my view, principally due to the lack of affordable housing in London. London weighting allowances – paying higher salaries for working in London as opposed to elsewhere in the UK – supposedly reflect the higher cost of living in the capital. However, many 'costs of living' are no higher in London than elsewhere in Britain. In fact food and fuel costs are lower in London than in many parts of Britain, including much of Scotland. The principal higher cost in London is housing and subsidising this through payment of London weightings is self-evidently counter-productive as a means of reducing London house prices and rents.

Job-seekers, attracted to London by the higher rates-of-pay on offer, simply increase the number of people seeking somewhere to live, thus pushing rents and house prices to even higher levels. London weightings also do nothing to benefit the UK economy outside London. While, in theory, an employer might be encouraged to locate a business in an area where workers will accept a lower rate of pay, in practice the best workers will be available in areas where pay rates are higher. Moreover, pay rates are only one of many considerations an employer has when deciding where to locate a business but will often be an employee's prime consideration when seeking a job. Consequently, it appears likely that London weightings have themselves contributed to the Capital's dominant position in the UK's economy.

Attempts to alleviate London's housing shortage by building garden cities and 'overspill' housing estates in the Home Counties have also contributed to its economic dominance, due to the agglomeration effect of concentrating a large population and their employing businesses in close proximity to each other. Experience thus suggests that the recent decision by the Coalition Government[70] to build more garden cities in this crowded corner of the country will do nothing to reduce the current north/south economic divide and is unlikely to make London housing any more affordable.

Previous Government interventions aiming to reduce the demand for homes in London have sought to move jobs to areas of high unemployment, either by dispersing existing London jobs or by creating entirely new jobs. While initially increasing employment opportunities in the target areas, neither intervention has succeeded in stemming the growth of the north/south economic divide.

Many of the dispersed jobs have been in public sector administration, with the governance of the dispersed functions remaining in London. Employees who progress into promoted posts are thus likely to be relocated to a London headquarters, thus increasing demand for housing in the Capital and maintaining low-wage economies elsewhere in Britain. In addition, the separation of governance and administration is likely to add to the overall costs of undertaking the work, thereby reducing the sustainability of the dispersed jobs.

---

[70] Locally-led Garden Cities, Department for Communities and Local Government, April 2014

Similarly, directing new businesses to locations which would not otherwise have been selected can result in increased costs for the employer, including workforce training, materials/components procurement and product distribution. Again this is likely to reduce the sustainability of the business as evidenced notoriously with the establishment of the Hillman Imp car plant in Linwood.

It surely follows that sustainable economic development outwith London and the South East is more likely to result from policies stimulating the organic growth of conditions in which business flourish and residents enjoy a good standard of living than from interventions which attempt to create these conditions artificially and often only for a limited period. The Party's adoption of policies which will allow businesses and residents to make their own life choices will not only constitute a better means of sustainably rebalancing Britain's economy than interventions like one-off grants and incentives like regional pay rates but will also uphold Liberal non-interventionist principles. To inform the development of these policies, it is necessary first to identify the factors responsible for London's economic prosperity and secondly to consider the extent to which these are – or could be – present in Britain's other conurbations.

First and foremost, London is the capital city of the United Kingdom. As such, it benefits not only from the kudos which attaches to any capital city but also from the fame and fortune accrued by the UK throughout its history and particularly during the years of the British Empire. As seat of the UK Government, London houses embassies from most of the world's states and the headquarters of countless companies that value ease of access to HM Government. These include the major banks and other businesses, whose presence has made the City of London one of the world's premier financial centres. The centrality of law in all trading activity and Britain's reputation for the administration of justice have, similarly, made London one of the world's leading legal centres.

Clearly, while London remains capital of the UK, there is no opportunity for other British cities to replicate this role. However, many capital cities are far less dominant economically than London. In the USA, for example, Washington is the seat of Government but New York dominates in economic terms. Similarly in Australia, the economies of both Sydney and Melbourne are larger than that of Canberra. Designation as a capital city is therefore not a pre-requisite for economic domination. Nevertheless, it is clear that any centre of governance has the potential to attract the headquarters of companies seeking opportunities to influence the policy makers.

It follows that economic activity and growth is likely to be better balanced in countries with a federal structure than in one with a single seat of government. This has been cited previously in support of proposals for the devolved administrations of Scotland and Wales and there is little doubt that the Liberal Democrat aspiration to devolve power to the English regions in a truly federal UK would assist in reducing the current north/south economic divide.

Consequently, it would appear that the first policy objective in rebalancing Britain's economy should be further devolution of governance, to the extent necessary for businesses based outwith London to be at no disadvantage to those based in the capital, as regards their ability to influence those responsible for policies impacting on them. The creation of employment opportunities outwith London through this devolution of governance could significantly reduce the need for new housing in London and the south east and moderate London's rate of house price inflation. At the same time, an increase in demand for housing in the conurbations outwith London could assist in their sustainable regeneration, providing an incentive to refurbish currently unoccupied houses.

The second factor central to London's economic dominance is agglomeration. London is fast becoming a city-state with all the activities required to run a successful economy located within its boundaries and immediate hinterland. The concentration of governance, administration, commerce, financial markets, legal practices etc. within a relatively compact area improves the efficiency of each activity and consequently attracts more businesses in each sector to locate within the London conurbation rather than elsewhere in the UK. This concentration of activity is, in turn, supported by a stable and increasingly skilled workforce, as employees are attracted by the range of job opportunities on offer in almost every sphere of economic activity.

It is not difficult to see how the agglomeration benefits currently enjoyed by London and the south east might be replicated elsewhere in the UK. There are already concentrations of population in the East and West Midlands which, taken together, match that of Greater London. An even larger conurbation could be created by combining the populations of all towns and cities in northern England (i.e. those centred on Manchester, Liverpool and Leeds). However, I do not believe that there is any particular significance regarding the current population of Greater London. The agglomeration benefits which have fuelled its economic growth kicked in when its population was much smaller than it is now.

There is thus no reason why England's readily identified conurbations – Northwest, Northeast, Yorkshire and Humberside, West Midlands and East Midlands – could not each benefit from their own agglomeration of activities. The populations and the range of activities already established in Scotland's Central Belt and the Newport-Cardiff-Swansea corridor similarly appear able to deliver agglomeration benefits. Why, then, are these benefits not already more in evidence? Principally, I would suggest, because the towns and cities within each of these conurbations currently function as separate entities, competing rather than collaborating with their neighbours.

The London conurbation has long been regarded as an entity, despite the often frosty relationships between the conurbation-wide local authority and the constituent London boroughs. As the conurbation expanded into the suburbs outwith the London County Council (LCC) boundary, the LCC was replaced by the Greater London Council (GLC) until abolished by Margaret Thatcher's government in 1986. It was soon recognised that the collection of central government bodies and joint boards created to undertake the strategic functions previously exercised by the GLC was less effective than a single conurbation-wide authority and, following a show of public support in a referendum, the Greater London Authority (GLA) was established in July 2000. The strategic approach to land use planning, property development and transport possible under the Mayor's leadership has undoubtedly been a contributing factor in London's recent economic growth.

I would therefore conclude that Britain's conurbations outwith London are unlikely to fully realise the benefits of agglomeration until regional authorities, similar to the GLA, assume responsibility for, at least, strategic planning and transport functions on a conurbation-wide basis. A policy to establish such authorities fits well with that to further devolve governance, suggested above.

The third and final factor necessary to replicate London's economic growth elsewhere in Britain is good connectivity. There is little doubt that London enjoys excellent connectivity both internally (between any two points within the conurbation) and externally (between the conurbation and other cities in Britain and abroad). Moreover, London's connectivity is set to improve still further: internally with the construction of Crossrail – a £15 billion heavy-rail line running east-west across the city, much of it underground – and externally with increased runway capacity planned for the south-east, the new London Gateway port and the HS2 high speed rail (HSR) line.

London was specifically excluded from the 1985 Act which deregulated bus services throughout the rest of the UK and which has made it practically impossible for local authorities outwith London to properly co-ordinate public transport provision. Although the provision of public transport within London has itself been subject to change since London Transport had direct operational responsibility for all bus and underground services, there has always been in place a single body to co-ordinate all modes of public transport on a conurbation-wide basis. This is currently the GLA, which not only plans and procures public transport services but also provides an integrated, cashless, payment system for these services – the Oyster card.

London's comprehensive local transport network maximises the agglomeration benefits discussed above. Businesses are able to draw on an extensive supply of skilled labour resident within easy reach of a reliable public transport connection to the workplace. And business trips within the conurbation can be undertaken efficiently, often by rail, allowing face-to-face meetings to be convened, at short notice if necessary, with professional advisors, service providers, clients and customers.

London's economic growth rate is unlikely to be replicated in Britain's other conurbations until they, too, have in place comprehensive public transport systems providing internal connectivity to match that in London. While it will not be possible, in the short term, to construct local rail networks as extensive as London's or to fund networks of franchised bus services to match that in the Capital, these should be aspirations. An immediate policy objective could be to establish conurbation-wide transport authorities and legislate for increased regional regulation of bus services. Each conurbation could then co-ordinate the provision of existing public transport services in a way that maximises its internal connectivity, while also facilitating the forward planning of the infrastructure and services required to deliver the degree of internal connectivity necessary to fully realise the conurbation's agglomeration benefits.

While it is possible, at least theoretically, for other conurbations to develop their internal connectivity to match that of London, it will not be easy for them to match London's exemplary external connectivity. The networks of roads and rail lines which connect London directly with every other urban centre in Britain are a legacy of London's long history as the UK's capital. Such is the radial nature of these networks that many urban areas are better connected to London than to other urban areas much closer to them. In addition, the Capital's external connectivity to Europe is better than that of Britain's other major conurbations, largely as a direct consequence of its geographical location close to the Straits of Dover. This proximity to the near Continent has become even more significant, as regards London's economic dominance of Britain, since the Channel Tunnel opened in 1994.

Prior to the construction of the 'Chunnel', all international passenger and goods traffic movements required the use of a ship or aircraft. Consequently, the international connectivity of each conurbation depended primarily on its proximity to a relevant sea port or airport. Liverpool and Glasgow were favoured sea-ports for transatlantic traffic, while Britain's North Sea ports provided convenient alternatives to the south coast ports for shipments to and from Europe. Similarly, for long-haul (especially transatlantic) flights, during much of the twentieth century Prestwick airport featured alongside Heathrow as a premier UK gateway. Consequently, international connectivity was much the same throughout Britain and rarely the deciding factor for business location.

Unfortunately, this is no longer the case. Developments across all modes of transport have combined to significantly improve London's connectivity to the rest of the world, while simultaneously reducing that of Britain's other conurbations. While the most obvious of these is London's direct rail connection to mainland Europe via the Channel Tunnel, there have also been important changes in the shipping and aviation industries.

The use of bigger ships and the containerisation of freight transport have necessitated the construction/modification of port facilities. As a result shipping activities have been rationalised, with new, deep-water, container-handling, facilities provided at a limited number of locations, chosen for their ability to generate a healthy economic return for their owners. Unsurprisingly, given London's economic dominance, Britain's two largest ports, Felixstowe and Southampton, are in southeast England and the newest, London Gateway in Essex, is just 25 miles from central London. While not the only deep-water ports in Britain capable of handling containerised traffic, this concentration of port capacity in southeast England can only strengthen the current north/south economic divide.

Similarly, as passenger jet planes have increased in size, the world's major airlines have concentrated their activities at a relatively small number of 'hub' airports to which they can attract the requisite number of passengers to fill a long-haul flight. Other airports – the majority – have been termed 'point-to-point' and handle flights on popular inter-city routes, where passenger numbers local to that airport are sufficient to fill the planes. Flights from point-to-point airports include those to hub airports where passengers transit for long-haul destinations.

Wherever possible, passengers will aim to avoid transiting and choose a single flight direct to their destination. Such flights are not only more convenient but more efficient, with several hours 'transit time' at an airport not uncommon. Any business heavily reliant on long-haul flights will therefore choose, if possible, a location close to a hub airport, so as to minimise any requirement for transiting to and from domestic point-to-point flights. Currently Britain's only hub airport is London Heathrow, further strengthening the economic dominance of London and the southeast.

It is clear that London's superior external connectivity is a significant factor in its economic supremacy. It follows that any attempt to rebalance Britain's economy must include measures to reduce the differential between the external connectivity of London and that of Britain's other conurbations. Connectivity's potential role in rebalancing Britain's economy has already been recognised by both the Coalition Government and Her Majesty's Opposition and is now cited as a major objective of the proposed high speed rail line, HS2.[71] However, the supporting documentation for HS2 claims only that "high speed rail could benefit thousands of businesses by improving (their) access to the huge and internationally-competitive markets of London and the south East".[72]

In other words HS2, as currently proposed, will only improve the external connectivity of cities on the HSR network to London and to each other. Crucially, all journeys to and from Europe will continue to involve a change of station in Central London. HS2 may actually

---

[71] DfT: The Strategic Case for HS2, Ministerial forward, October 2013

[72] DfT: High Speed Rail, Investing in Britain's Future, page 12, February 2011

increase London's economic dominance as workers commute by HSR over longer distances to even more jobs in London. This is a lost opportunity; appropriately planned and implemented, HS2 could most certainly assist in rebalancing Britain's economy.

Equally disappointing is Sir Howard Davies' interim report on the Airport Commission's examination of how the UK's status as a leading global aviation hub can be maintained. This concludes, contrary to current Liberal Democrat policy, that new runways should be provided at either Heathrow or Gatwick airports.[73] This will do nothing to rebalance Britain's economy or to boost the UK's hub status, with Paris and Schiphol continuing as convenient hub airports for much of northern Britain. It follows that revisions to both the current proposals for HS2 and the conclusions of the Airports Commission are essential if improved external connectivity is to assist in rebalancing Britain's economy and delivering geographical justice.

HS2's current proposals have not proved popular with the public, primarily, I suspect, because they appear to provide additional capacity at greater cost (both financial and environmental) than obviously necessary, while the time savings delivered by HSR over the relatively short distances between adjacent stations are not considered worthwhile. Many engineering professionals are now calling for a review of the project, the majority favouring the provision of additional capacity at conventional speeds. I would argue otherwise; for a more extensive network of dedicated HSR lines as the best means of providing both additional capacity and also a step-change in connectivity.

The current proposals for HS2 have been developed following Network Rail's forecast that by 2020 the West Coast Main Line (WCML), particularly at its southern end,

---

[73] Airports Commission: Interim Report, December 2013

will effectively be full to capacity.[74] Both Network Rail and the then Labour Government[75] concluded that a new High Speed Rail (HSR) line would constitute the best means of providing the additional capacity required. However, while Network Rail proposed a single HSR line between London and Scotland, exploiting the potential of HSR to significantly reduce journey times over longer distances, attracting modal shift from air travel, and consequently demonstrating a high Benefit:Cost Ratio (BCR), HS2 propose[76] a 'Y' network extending northwards from Central London only as far as Manchester and Leeds, with far less potential to significantly reduce journey times. Immediately south of these two cities, HS2 propose connections to the existing West and East Coast Main Lines, with onward travel, to Glasgow and Edinburgh respectively, using specially designed and built 'classic-compatible' trains.

HS2's proposals mirror French practice, where high speed trains run beyond the extent of HSR, at slower speeds, on existing railway lines. They appealed to the British Government in that they could be presented to the electorate as bringing high speed trains into most major cities in the UK without the need for an extensive network of new HSR lines. However, since only those cities on the new 'Y' network would benefit from true high speed services and significant journey-time reductions, the overall BCR of HS2's proposals is only marginally positive. Consequently, in developing these proposals, relatively small differences in journey time on the faster HSR section proved critical and resulted in the early elimination of many potential route alignments and London station sites for HS2, in favour of a

---

[74] Network Rail: Meeting the capacity challenge: The case for new lines, August 2009
[75] Department for Transport: High Speed Rail - Command Paper, March 2010
[76] Department for Transport: High Speed Rail - Command Paper, March 2010

direct route through the Chiltern Hills terminating at Euston station.

Among the London station sites eliminated was Stratford, where a triangular arrangement of tracks, similar to that currently proposed for the HS2 junction east of Birmingham, would enable HSR trains from the north to be routed either westwards into the current HS1 terminal at St Pancras or south-eastwards to the Channel Tunnel. In the reverse direction trains arriving from Europe could run either into London (St Pancras) or directly via HS2 to other British cities. While it is unlikely that passenger numbers would justify the operation of more than one direct service per day each way between Europe and any conurbation other than London, passengers from other conurbations finding the timing of these direct services unsuitable would still have the option of joining London's European services at Stratford or St Pancras.

Terminating HS2 at Stratford instead of London (Euston) would avoid the need for disruptive demolition and tunnelling in Camden and a rebuild (for HSR) of Euston station. It would also avoid disruption during construction to WCML services at Euston. Minor changes and additions to the Crossrail proposals would allow passengers to interchange at Stratford between it and both HS1 and HS2 services instead of at Old Oak Common as currently proposed. The most cost-effective route for HS2 between Stratford and Birmingham is likely to avoid the Chiltern Hills, thereby removing a significant number of objections to HS2. Most importantly, facilitating direct rail services between Europe and each of Britain's major conurbations could kick-start a rebalancing of the British economy.

However, this rebalancing is unlikely to materialise unless continuous HSR tracks, capable of carrying the larger gauge rolling stock used in Europe, link Stratford to each of Britain's major conurbations. HS2's proposals to extend the reach of HSR services by running classic-compatible trains over existing tracks should therefore be abandoned in favour of procuring only 'captive', continental-gauge, HSR rolling stock to run solely on dedicated HSR lines and into purpose-built HSR stations. Inter alia, this would eliminate the potential for accidents similar to those that have already occurred in Europe, as a result of HSR trains using conventional lines and stations at inappropriate speeds.

A consequence of facilitating direct rail services between each of Britain's conurbations and Europe is that each HSR station in Britain will require immigration and customs officers, if 'de-training' at an intermediate station in Kent is to be avoided. The former is much preferred and should be possible, provided that comparatively few HSR stations are built. HSR stations should therefore be located where they can facilitate interchange to multiple services on existing lines serving a wide range of destinations.

Ideally, the first phase of HS2 should link Stratford and Crewe, where cross-platform interchange could be provided to all northern destinations on the existing WCML. Thereafter, the early completion of dedicated HSR tracks between London and Scotland should be a priority. Additional HSR stations should be built only at locations providing interchange with sufficient classic services to generate the patronage required to fill a high speed train running non-stop to a single destination, thereby maximising the time-saving benefits of HSR. While fewer stations will be served directly by high speed trains than currently proposed by HS2, a greater proportion of Britain's population is likely to use a high speed train for at least part of their journey.

Each of the suggested changes to HS2's current proposals is anticipated to reduce costs. A route avoiding the Chilterns should require fewer tunnels. Use of only continental-gauge rolling stock will avoid the higher costs of designing and building classic-compatible trains. Use of existing London HSR stations (Stratford and St Pancras) will avoid the costs of rebuilding Euston and tunnelling into it, while costs will also be reduced by building or adapting fewer stations to accommodate HSR services. It is appreciated that these cost savings will be matched or exceeded by increasing the size of the HSR network but the outcome will be game-changing.

A dedicated HSR network will be able to operate to the precise timetable required without the potential for disruption caused by delays on existing lines. All conurbations will be within 2½ hours' travel time of each other and travel on the HSR network will be an option for all long distance rail journeys in Britain. Most importantly, HSR services will connect each of Britain's conurbations directly to those in continental Europe.

Ideally, to replicate London's international connectivity for passenger travel involving a long-haul flight, a hub airport should be equally accessible from all Britain's conurbations. However, to avoid reducing London's connectivity, the aim must be, instead, either to maximise Heathrow's accessibility to other conurbations or to ensure that any new hub airport is no further from central London as regards door-to-door travel time than Heathrow is currently. Given that a hub airport requires at least three runways (Birmingham has room for four) and it is Liberal Democrat policy to build no more runways in southeast England, Birmingham appears the obvious location for a replacement hub airport for Britain.

Birmingham's current airport is understood to have room for expansion and is closer to Britain's other conurbations than Heathrow. For those in the capital, the time taken to travel non-stop between Birmingham International airport and central London by HSR should be little different to that using the current Heathrow express rail service via Paddington. Crucially, passengers from other conurbations can access Birmingham airport without the need to travel through central London. Birmingham is already the hub of Britain's motorway network and is well-placed to form the hub of a new HSR network. To maximise the use of land-based transport modes for trips between the hub airport and Britain's conurbations, the hub should be the only British airport with a HSR station.

Finally, increasing economic activity in areas like Scotland, Manchester and the North East, should make viable point-to-point flights from their local airports to more destinations than at present removing the requirement for transiting, while HSR to Britain's hub airport (Heathrow or Birmingham) should release more slots at the hub for connecting flights to places like Aberdeen and the Scottish Islands.

In this essay, I have identified three factors that I consider key to securing geographical justice for Britain; namely devolution of governance, the establishment of conurbation-wide strategic authorities and improved connectivity. These could translate into the following manifesto commitments:

1. Work towards devolving, to six or seven English regions, powers similar to those already devolved to Scotland, Wales and Northern Ireland.

2. Legislate to establish, in each major conurbation, a single authority with responsibility for all strategic functions including land use planning and transport.

3. Legislate for greater regulation of local bus services outwith London, to enable strategic transport authorities to fully co-ordinate the provision of public transport services.

4. Undertake an immediate review of the current proposals for HS2, with a view to maximising HSR's potential to rebalance Britain's economy, reducing rail journey times

and carbon emissions, while providing additional rail capacity.

5. Re-affirm opposition to any new airport capacity in southeast England and refuse to be bound by the outcome of the Airport Commission's current examination of how the UK's status as a leading global aviation hub can be maintained.

Conclusion

The Challenge for Liberals

Nigel Lindsay and John Barrett

In the hours and days after the next election, Liberal Democrats will have to take urgent decisions, the consequences of which may determine whether the Party survives as a mass political organization or not. The radical voice of the Party, which is the main reason many joined it, and whose recent absence has been the reason so many thousands have left it, will need to be reasserted powerfully during the General Election and from the first days of the new parliament.

The essays in this book point the way to how this may be done. They challenge the view that there is now a consensus of the right. They show that Liberalism is a radical philosophy, that the inequalities developing in our state have a corrosive effect on everyone and that there is an electoral space waiting for radical Liberals to fill it. They demonstrate that human rights and civil liberties need defenders today more than at any time in the last six decades, and that the poorest people in the country need support rather than the routinely degrading treatment meted out to them by recent governments. And they challenge the flow of power and resources from the most remote and sparsely-populated areas to the power centres and international companies situated mostly in or near London.

Themes for the Future

In her essay, Caron Lindsay rightly suggests that "theme based thinking should replace our traditional way of writing a manifesto: picking a Government department and putting a list of policies underneath it". The policies, she points out, should be there as evidence of the values they represent. This book sets out the philosophy on which those values are based, and gives examples of the values which can be derived from that philosophy and how they can be translated into radical policies that can modernize and improve our country.

What should be our themes? The evidence of this book is that they should include economic justice, geographical justice, civil liberties and human rights, internationalism, the removal of barriers to meaningful political participation by ordinary people, a leadership that listens to the people and the party, and a reassertion of the radical Liberal voice in British politics.

A new Capitalism

A move towards economic justice will involve inventing a new capitalism that improves the incomes and capacities of the poorest people in Britain, and reduces the undeserved and frequently self-assigned privileges of the super-rich. As Prateek Buch, Robert Brown and others have shown, a start must be made by a revolution in the way banks work, so that they serve the common good rather than the interests of a very few individuals. Despite all that has happened over the past seven or eight years, the banks and other financial institutions remain much as they were. Despite multi-million pound fines paid by banks for wrongdoing, no individual was apparently responsible, for none has been jailed. The opportunity to use government shareholdings and financial influence to change them has not been exploited in the way it might have been.

A new kind of capitalism will involve an acceptance that the housing market must not be artificially boosted to provide temporary, pre-election booms which distort the economy and consume resources that could instead be invested in ways that would help the wider economy. It will involve investing much more of our GDP in research and investment than we do at present. It will involve a recognition that manufacturing industry has suffered disproportionately in many parts of the UK over the last decade, but that well-directed government support for innovation will help it generate more jobs and make a stronger contribution to our economy.

We suggest that in developing a new capitalism, Liberal legislators should look critically at some aspects of commercial law in this country, much of which developed in a different age, and sometimes seems designed to protect the interests of the haves, rather than the have-nots. The law controlling joint stock banks failed to prevent the near collapse of several British banks in 2007-2008 and so needs to be re-examined. We need to consider whether it should discourage banks from funding gigantic takeovers which facilitate asset-stripping and are not justified by any definition of sustainable public interest. Limited liability law allows companies to walk away from their debts, sometimes even re-forming a few days later with a new set of directors. The law obstructs attempts to discover the beneficial owners of shares in companies doing business in our high streets and on our football pitches and, as Prateek Buch points out elsewhere in this volume, we do not even have the power to call to account those who run our pension and endowment schemes for their votes on matters like excessive executive pay. Tax laws permit international companies to choose to pay tax on profits generated in the UK in other, laxer jurisdictions. The UK permits Jersey, Guernsey, and the Isle of Man to operate as tax havens, just as other EU member states permit similar services to be offered to their citizens by micro-states such as Andorra, Monaco and Liechtenstein. There may be justifications for such favourable treatment given by the law to those who have most but, if so, they should not go unchallenged. Neither the Labour nor Conservative parties have any appetite to make that challenge, so these privileges will continue to be unquestioned unless Liberals start making intelligent enquiries about them.

We need particularly to expect that there will be forceful opposition to any such moves, and we need the sense to work out in advance how to counter these. One element of this is that ministers and would-be ministers need to be certain of what they wish to achieve before they take office. They need to be firmly enough rooted in Liberal values and know enough about their subject to stick to their policies and resist the blandishments of Sir Humphrey in the civil service, or Lady ----- at a dinner party. This has not always seemed to be the case since 2010. Liberal Democrat members have too often been bemused by policy U-turns by MPs once they become ministers. This difficulty has sometimes been exacerbated by a failure to explain.

Reducing Inequalities

Robert Aldridge has shown how a new and more Liberal capitalism should recognise and address the needs of those who rely on state benefits. Duncan Exley's contribution, and the work of the Spirit Level Foundation, show clearly how everyone is harmed when inequalities increase as support is withdrawn from those who have least. We need to rekindle the determination shown by the great reforming governments of Asquith and Attlee, to pass legislation that will ensure all our people have a level of income which enables them to live fulfilling lives. Prateek Buch has pointed out that a thriving, sustainable economy is not an end in itself but that for Liberals its primary purpose should be "to empower all citizens to secure for themselves the means with which to live fulfilling lives they have reason to value".

Reducing the privileges of the greediest members of society will not in itself help the less affluent, but it will contribute to the Liberal purpose of reducing inequality in Britain. We need to find ways to reduce the agglomeration of wealth in London, and to bring an end to the fairy-tale salaries granted to each other by those at the top of the financial services and some other industries.

Equal Voices

The most satisfactory way to reduce economic inequality, though, is by increasing political equality. If politicians of all parties believed that young, un(der)employed, and otherwise disadvantaged people were going to vote in their own interests in the same proportions as older, more affluent people, the nature of politics in Britain would probably start to change. There would be a greater likelihood of that happening if we could provide conditions that encouraged meaningful participation in the political life of the country by the less well-off, as hinted above. Again there is an opportunity for Liberal Democrats to lead the way in providing meaningful debate about the issues that matter, and eschewing the sound-bite culture so beloved of advisers who are often far removed from the needs and aspirations of most ordinary people.

As well as seeking to increase people's capacity to get involved in, and influence, political debate, we need to return to the principle that every citizen has a single vote and that these votes are each of equal value. A claim that is still made about our democracy, this has become less and less true in recent years. The lack of a proper Senate to replace the unaccountable House of Lords is an obvious example of this, as is the power of City wealth that flows to the political parties in the interest of protecting privilege. Another is the undermining of the secret ballot. The value of one person's vote is reduced if money or undue pressure can obtain twenty votes cast the other way. The wider availability of postal votes has already been shown to lead to bundles of votes being given in some English cities under duress or perhaps even without being seen by those to whom they belonged. Proposals to vote by text or over the internet only increase the opportunity for such corruption. Making an annual trip of a few hundred yards to a polling station is not a great hardship for most voters who are keen to express a preference, but where the need arises to make it easier to vote, then this must be done in a way that is consistent with protecting the right of every voter to choose in secret.

A fundamental of equality is equality of rights, covered so ably in Robert Brown's contribution to this book. Incorporation of the European Convention of Human Rights into law was a step of great significance, but Liberal Democrats have been silent as some of these rights have been whittled away by anti-terrorist legislation. The fundamental principle that a person is deemed innocent until proven guilty has been undermined by legislation said to be aimed at terrorism but in reality affecting us all. For an innocent person's phone and e-mail use to be monitored and stored is an affront almost as serious as storage of the DNA of innocent people. It is unlikely that any terrorist would use phones or e-mail to transact their business when powers of interception are so well-known – they will surely find other means, while the private communications of millions of innocent citizens are spied on and recorded by a state, whose control apparatus may at a point in the future be less well-disposed than it is now.

Energy

Another of our themes should be energy use and production (probably in that order). Many Liberal Democrats consider the environment a key issue and a reason to support the party. Many of those same supporters have serious concerns about building new nuclear power plants and about fracking, and are committed to increasing the amount of renewables used for electricity production. So when the Liberal Democrat Energy Secretary, Ed Davey, signed a deal to support a new nuclear power plant at Hinckley B in Somerset, it was more than a surprise to many in the party. Despite his long term antipathy to nuclear power, he agreed to guarantee EDF (a state-owned company, just not owned by our state) an inflation proofed electricity price for 35 years to build that nuclear power station. The Treasury is also offering to underwrite most of the £16bn loans needed for the project.

The coalition agreement states that Liberal Democrats will speak against nuclear power stations and then they will abstain on any vote. The Conservative policy is that they will only support nuclear power stations if they require no public subsidy. Ed Davey has therefore signed up for a policy that is not Liberal Democrat policy, is not Conservative policy, and is not even endorsed in the coalition agreement. Similar fault lines have appeared in the party on the issue of fracking, which is embraced by our ministers despite widespread scepticism among party members. Where the Liberal Democrats stand on such issues is a puzzle, even for Liberal Democrat members.

We need to go back to first principles on energy policy. A good start could be made by thinking about how much energy we as a country are entitled to use, bearing in mind the needs of people in other countries and the needs of generations yet unborn. From that start, we could design ways of meeting that target by reducing consumption and generating more energy from sustainable sources, many of which (such as tidal energy) are so far virtually untapped.

Foreign Policy

Under the leadership of Charles Kennedy, support for the Liberal Democrats grew significantly because our foreign policy was related to principles to which we adhered in the face of often vitriolic criticism. The principled and united stand of the party opposing military action in Iraq, when over a million people took to the streets, gained the party many new members and supporters, especially former Labour voters.

This was in stark contrast to the 2013 vote in Parliament paving the way for military action in Syria, which was supported by the party leadership, but opposed by the majority of members and most MPs from all parties in Parliament, and finally resulted in a Government defeat, with the Lib Dems being split on the issue. Some Liberal Democrat MPs were telephoned and arm-twisted to support the government position on military action out of loyalty to Nick Clegg. What a contrast to the principled and united stand on Iraq!

If the vote had been carried and military action had followed, the party would have ended up on the same side as the Islamist fanatics of ISIS who are now causing terror in much of the Middle East. The whole fiasco suggests that the leadership and members of the parliamentary party need to think more about how Liberal values should guide them on foreign affairs, what lessons could have been learnt from the ultimately disastrous intervention in Libya a couple of years earlier, and the value of listening to the party outside parliament.

Such an approach would involve applying Liberal principles to the relationships between nations, just as between people. It is no longer our role to intervene routinely in conflicts on other continents, whether or not more powerful allies are doing so. We need to shed the last vestiges of colonial attitudes. Perhaps we also need to find ways to reduce our economic dependence on the defence industries and the arms trade. Importantly, we need to remember that Europe does not end at the boundaries of the EU. Russia is part of our continent, and we need to live with it. We need to find better ways of resolving its security concerns and our own, than by tit-for-tat measures that end up hurting both sides.

Re-asserting the radical voice in UK Politics

Re-discovering the radical voice of Liberalism is important not just for the Party, but for the health of our democracy. The Conservatives moved to the right in the mid-1970s. The Labour Party followed fifteen or twenty years later, under Tony Blair. The consensus between the Conservatives and New Labour which resulted meant that people with progressive views were under-represented in parliament. Only Liberals spoke for those (sometimes the majority) who were uneasy about the consensus on such issues as joining the USA to invade Iraq, and the creeping curtailment of civil liberties. The rightward movement of the LibDem leadership over the past six years has opened an electoral gap to the left of centre, and has left many feeling that no-one now speaks for them in parliament.

The challenges to society and politics in Britain and Scotland today will not be solved by another term of Conservative-led government, however much posturing there is about some undefined "fairness". Conservatives seek, as they always have done, to increase the power and wealth of an elite which is already absurdly affluent. How would it be otherwise, when the major donors to their party funds are "shipping magnates, hedge fund managers, cash-and-carry barons, investment bankers, and Russian tycoons" (paying guests at a 2014 Conservative fund-raising evening, listed in *The Guardian*). No party funded in this way is going to speak with a radical voice or bring greater social justice to Britain. Caron Lindsay points out in her essay that Liberals and Conservatives are fundamental opposites, just as WS Gilbert did 133 years ago in *Iolanthe* –

> *...every boy and every gal*
> *That's born into the world alive*
> *Is either a little Liberal*
> *Or else a little Conservative*

The Labour Party long ago gave up any pretence to being a party of radical reform, and has shown itself scared to speak out against the ideas of conservatism.

We need to promote our own radical agenda, and refuse to be drawn into debate on the selective priorities of newspapers with a right-wing agenda and the broadcasters who follow their lead. One reason why many abstainers do not vote is that electoral debate in the media focuses on issues that are far from their immediate concern. We must try to change that. A way of doing so will be, as Robert Brown has hinted, to lose the party's addiction to "positioning", based on the use of private polling and focus groups, and instead start to lead public opinion by standing for what we believe in. Polling can yield valuable information, but of course it gives the same information to all users. Positioning the party on the basis of such feedback inevitably leads to it competing with the other parties for the same tiny electoral space, while overlooking the needs and wishes of the millions who do not form part of the presumed centre.

This is just one example of a retreat from radicalism. Many voters believe that the party has given in to pressure too often. Saying that it has stopped the extremes of the Conservatives and given people an increased tax threshold has to be set against its support for unpopular welfare reform proposals, tax cuts for the wealthy, the tuition fees debacle and much more. There is little understanding in the party south of the border that NHS reform in England, if done badly, will have an adverse electoral impact in Scotland, where protecting the NHS is a key issue for the voters.

We need to lead public opinion, as we did over Iraq, and not follow it. And we need to stand by the principles of Liberalism in foreign affairs, on energy and health, on education, and in all other fields. When trust has gone, or people assume the party is not telling the truth, it becomes impossible to regain that trust by words or promises in manifestos or other publications. Actions may convince electors the party is on the right course but, with fewer people elected at all levels and fewer members to campaign in local communities, this has inevitably become more of a problem for us.

People in many areas can no longer say they have a good hard-working local Liberal Democrat Councillor, MSP, or AM to show that on the ground the party represents them well, as many of those individuals have now gone. When Councillors, MSPs, and AMs have lost their seats, many long term local activists follow them and give up as well. Unless something significant changes before the General Election, it may well be that those Liberal Democrat MPs who manage to hold on to their seats at that election will be a few popular locally well-known individuals, as thirty years ago, but without a significant level of public support or a truly national party behind them. The numbers elected at the next election might result in a second coalition and the leadership may consider that returning to Government is the true measure of success for the party. They will, however, be on their own.

We should learn from the example of the German Liberals (FDP) that voters are not impressed by a party whose main aim seems to be keeping its leaders in government. We are much more likely to do well by speaking out as Britain's radical voice, and developing our historic role in leading public opinion with new, daring and radical ideas. That purpose can often be fulfilled as well in opposition as in government, as is pointed out elsewhere in this book.

This book suggests a better way forward by setting out the components of what we believe should be an identifiably radical and Liberal approach to politics after 2015. We need to assert and push such a programme, whether we are in government or in opposition, in order to re-fashion the Liberal Democrats for the people. If that does not happen, and the Party seems to project just an apologetic version of conservatism, the result will be entirely predictable. As with the Lib-Con coalitions of 1918-1922, and of the 1930s, our parliamentary numbers will be slashed, organization in the country will vanish, and a catastrophic split in the party is likely to be unavoidable. We believe we have shown that such an outcome can be avoided by projecting a new and radical Liberal identity, based on the principles laid out so clearly by Nigel Dower at the start of this book and developed into practical political approaches by our other contributors. The ideas are here, the journey has been mapped out and it is now time for us to get moving.

About the Contributors

Robert Aldridge was Edinburgh's youngest councillor when he was first elected as a Scottish Liberal thirty years ago. He is now one of the city's longest-serving councillors and was Leader of the Liberal Democrat group from 1997–99. He held the Environment brief during the LibDem/SNP administration of 2007–11. Robert is widely recognised as an expert on poverty and social exclusion issues. He is the Chief Executive of Homeless Action Scotland and is active in FEANTSA, the European federation of national homelessness organisations. He was a member of the Homelessness Task Force, set up in 1999 by the Scottish Executive, whose proposals and recommendations achieved the most progressive legislation on homelessness in Europe.

John Barrett is the former Liberal Democrat Member of Parliament for Edinburgh West. He has been a member of the Liberal Party and Liberal Democrats for over 30 years and was formerly an Edinburgh City Councillor. He is currently President of both The Scottish Liberal Club and Edinburgh West Liberal Democrats.

Robert Brown obtained First Class Honours in Law at Aberdeen University in 1965. Qualifying as a solicitor, he served a period as Procurator Fiscal Depute in Dumbarton, before joining a large Glasgow legal firm where he became senior civil partner. In 1977, Robert Brown was elected as the first Liberal Councillor in modern times in Glasgow, and remained undefeated until he stood down in 1992. He served as Liberal Democrat MSP for Glasgow from 1999 to 2011, and as Deputy Minister for Education from 2005 to 2007. From 2008–11, he was spokesperson on Justice and Civil Liberties in the Scottish Parliament. Since 2012, Robert has been a Councillor on South Lanarkshire Council. Robert served 10 years as Policy Convener of the Scottish Liberal Democrats, being responsible for a number of Party manifestos. He was Vice Chair of the Steel Commission on Moving to Federalism and a member of both Campbell Commissions on Home Rule and Community Rule.

Dr Prateek Buch contributes to Liberal Democrat policy as a member of the party's Federal Policy Committee and as Director of the Social Liberal Forum. He has commented extensively on political economy and health policy in the New Statesman, Independent Voices, the Guardian and Liberal Democrat Voice. Following a decade researching gene therapy for sight loss, Prateek is starting *Evidence Matters* – a campaign for the effective and transparent use of evidence in public policy – as part of the charity Sense About Science

Nigel Dower is Honorary Senior Lecturer in Philosophy at the University of Aberdeen, Scotland, where he taught for most of the period 1967–2004. He has also been a visiting professor a number of times in America and Iceland. He now acts as an academic consultant on 'Cosmopolitan agendas – exploring ethics in a globalized world'. He was President of the International Development Ethics Association from 2002 to 2006. His research interests in the last twenty years have focussed on various issues in global ethics, including development, the environment, human rights, peace & security, and global citizenship. His publications include *World Ethics – the New Agenda* (1998),

Introduction to Global Citizenship (2003) and *The Ethics of War and Peace* (2009). In 2007 he received an Honorary Doctorate (TD) from the University of Uppsala for his work on global ethics and related issues.

Duncan Exley is Director of The Equality Trust, an organisation that works to improve the quality of life in the UK by reducing economic inequality. Founded in 2009 by Bill Kerry, Richard Wilkinson and Kate Pickett, the launch of the organisation coincided with the publication of *The Spirit Level: Why more equal societies almost always do better,* a seminal study on the damaging effects of inequality on society.

Ross Finnie is a Chartered Accountant by profession and worked for nearly thirty years in the financial services sector. He joined the Scottish Liberal Party in 1964. He has served on the national executive and was Chair of the Scottish Liberal Party from 1982 to 1986. He was a local councillor in Inverclyde for twenty two years from 1977 to 1999. Ross was a Member of the Scottish Parliament from 1999–2011 and was the Cabinet Minister for Rural Affairs from 1999–2001 and for the Environment and Rural Development 2001–2007. Currently he is Chair of Scottish Environment Link, a Scottish Water Commissioner and a member of NHS Greater Glasgow & Clyde.

Gillian Gloyer held various positions in the Scottish Young Liberals throughout the 1980s, including Chairperson from 1985–87. She is currently Convenor of Edinburgh North-East and Leith Liberal Democrats. She is an expert on Albania, having worked there for four years directing a long-term training programme with young political party activists and, subsequently, researched and written *Albania: the Bradt Travel Guide,* the only serious English-language guidebook to the country. She has run voter education programmes, trained national and international election observers, advised national election commissions and observed electoral processes in Africa, the Middle East, Latin America, the former Soviet Union and the Balkans.

Tony Hughes is a Chartered Civil Engineer. After working in London and Dubai, he held the position of Transport Policy and Planning Manager with Glasgow City Council until his retirement in 2013. Tony co-ordinated the development and opening of Scotland's first long distance cycle route from Glasgow to Loch Lomond in 1989, and developed the City's Local Transport Strategy. He worked with City of Edinburgh Council on lobbying for Scotland's inclusion in the UK's High Speed Rail network.

Caron Lindsay joined the SDP on her 16th birthday in 1983. Since then she has held various offers at local and national level. She is currently Treasurer of the Scottish Liberal Democrats and a member of the Federal Executive. She is also co-editor of Liberal Democrat Voice.

Nigel Lindsay (no relation) was Director of a rural development agency in Lincolnshire before joining the Scottish Executive, where his work involved European funding for economic development. Soon after graduating MA and M.Litt from the University of Aberdeen he became the first Liberal member of Aberdeen city council in modern times. Fourteen years later, Liberals took control of the council and he became its convener of leisure and recreation. With Robert Brown and others, he led the successful campaign to have Jo Grimond elected rector of Aberdeen University. He is now a member of the University's Business Committee, and is Treasurer of the European Movement in Scotland.

Willis Pickard was editor of the Times Educational Supplement Scotland and has published a biography of the Scottish Victorian Liberal Duncan McLaren. He was Rector of Aberdeen University and is a former convener of the Scottish Liberal Club. He is currently chair of the Scottish branch of Liberal International Great Britain.

David Steel (Lord Steel of Aikwood) was brought up in Scotland and Kenya and graduated in law at the University of Edinburgh. He was a Borders MP for 32 years, Leader of the Liberal Party from 1976–1988, and a member of the House of Lords since 1997. He co-chaired the cross-party Scottish Constitutional Convention which devised the scheme for the Scottish Parliament, and was the first Presiding Officer of the Scottish Parliament from 1999–2003. He chaired the Scottish Liberal Democrat Commission which produced the ground breaking Steel Commission Report (*Moving to Federalism – A New Settlement for Scotland*) in March 2006.

Kate Stephen is a Liberal Democrat member of Highland Council, representing the Culloden and Ardersier Ward, and has been selected as the Liberal Democrat candidate for the Scottish Parliament constituency of Skye, Lochaber and Badenoch for the 2016 Scottish elections. Most of Kate's family come from the Isle of Skye and she has spent most of her life in the Highlands and Islands.

Sir Graham Watson is President of the Alliance of Liberals and Democrats for Europe, a party with members from 37 countries across the European continent. From 1994–2014 he served as a Member of the European Parliament for South West England and Gibraltar; during this period he chaired the EP's justice and home affairs committee (1999–2002) and led Parliament's Liberal Democrat Group (2002–09). He is the author of ten books on Liberalism, including *Building a Liberal Europe* (John Harper Publishing, 2011). He is married to Dr Rita Giannini; they have two grown-up children and divide their time between Langport and Brussels.